My Path to Identity

Marcia Hadfield

ISBN 979-8-89145-821-5 (paperback)

Cover design by Layken Davey—
www.instagram.com/laykendavey/

Dedication

Fifty-two years of this story were lived in the context of my immediate family. One husband and three children created the environment for my inner transformation. I am eternally grateful for their love that gave me the space and stability to discover who God is and who I am. Thank you, Robin, Duane, Heather, and Alicia.

Table of Contents

Introduction

Many, many years ago, I sat down at my dining room table in Christchurch, New Zealand, to research, reflect and write on my journey in relationships. I had lived long enough to realize this matter of relationship was not easily navigated. I had enjoyed many healthy relationships over the years, but many disappointing and sometimes downright devastating relationships had left me confused and raw inside. I needed to get my head around the answers to several questions:

- What was relationship?

- Where did it come from?

- Why was it so critical to living life?

- How were we to "do life" together with someone else?

That dining room table became my workshop, prayer closet, and workout room for more than a year. I went there right after breakfast with pen, paper, and Bible in hand. This was before the Internet and PCs. I stayed there until my kids came home from school.

I knew that I had to start with God because all relationships begin there—with God—then consider

relationships with myself and others; so, I went to the book that talks about the beginning of all things, the Bible—specifically Genesis 1:26 and 27. I learned much that year and wrote it all down:

- What does it mean to be made in God's image?

- Why did God create male and female?

- What was the core issue in Satan's offer to eat of the tree of the knowledge of good and evil?

- What does relationship look like?

- What are barriers to relationship?

- How do truth and love function in relationship?

- What does truth look like?

I never got to what love looks like, perhaps because truth was easier to explore and express. It's a strong component in my DNA mix. I lean to truth before I lean to love. But also, so much had already been written on love; I didn't know if I had anything new to add to the narrative. That's where I got stuck. I never finished; my manuscript got filed away, waiting until I had something meaningful to say about love.

INTRODUCTION

It is now some thirty years later, and I am again sitting at a dining room table, this time in Duvall, Washington, USA, and this time pecking a PC keyboard. In the years that have passed since my initial search, I've realized that identity is the core foundation of all relationships, whether with God, myself, or others. Who I am (identity) is what I bring into a relationship and a major determining factor of how that relationship will be journeyed and what it will look like along the way. Who I am begins with God…how He created me and why He created me. How I relate to Creator God and respond to Him determines how I see myself. How I see myself has a significant impact on all my relationships. So, identity is a big deal!

I have found that having a true understanding of God and myself (who I am) requires a journey of mountaintops and valleys. It is in the highs and lows of life that I touch the reality of who God is and who I am. So, let me share my journey, inviting you to travel those highs and lows with me and hear about what I learned along the way. I hope you'll see your own journey in mine and find wholeness and freedom in who you are because of who God is.

Bible Belt Heritage

My mother was a young war-time bride of twenty-one when she gave birth to her first child, Jack William. Fourteen months later, she gave birth to me; thirteen months after that, she brought my brother Richard into the world. Two years later, the Second World War was over, and my mother boarded a train with the three of us in tow to move from Kansas to California. My dad was out of the Navy and earning a living as a butcher in a Safeway grocery store.

We lived in government housing during my childhood years; it was there my brothers and I discovered the wider world of people our own age. The housing was framed in a quad. Four long single-story buildings, each housing four separate family units, bordered the quad. In the middle of the quad was a grassy plot of land. Adjacent and up a slight incline was another set of four buildings with its own grassy plot of land; somehow or another, our plot of land became the playground for every kid in those eight buildings. And there were many—we were the baby boomer generation.

My Path to Identity

That plot of land was where we made our forts, played hide-and-seek, divvied into teams for baseball games, broke an occasional window, and learned how to get along. My mom had an ironclad rule we didn't dare break: if one can't play, none of you can play. That one rule short-circuited a lot of arguments and hurt feelings, but it did more. It told us who we were…we were family, and family sticks together! On that playground, we became the Three Musketeers who stuck together through thick and thin.

Those years were wholesome years. My aunts and uncles and grandparents lived close by, so we often gathered with extended family. A favorite was getting up early on a Sunday morning to head to the mountains for the day. It always started with brewing coffee, frying bacon and eggs on the camp stove, and devouring homemade cinnamon rolls. We kids played in the stream, and the adults just shook off their cares with outdoor living for a few hours. Those days were family at its best. We also enjoyed birthday parties, Thanksgiving feasts, going to Grandma's for her biscuits, coleslaw, and devil's food cake or spending Christmas together opening presents and eating homemade fudge and divinity candy.

All of that changed two months after my seventh birthday. There were four of us kids by then; my sister

Cindy was born just a month before I turned seven. It was Thanksgiving weekend, and we kids were all hustled off to relatives for a few days. I remember the telephone ringing, then hushed voices around me. My dad had died a day after brain surgery at thirty-three years of age. My mother was left with four children ages eight, seven, six, and three months. I don't recall any of us crying; we just seemed to accept it as something that was. I do remember that on the day of the funeral reception at our house, we kids went to the theater nearby to watch "Look for the Silver Lining."

My family's very settled world had suddenly become unsettled. Mom was thrust back into the workforce, and my siblings and I were looked after by a caregiver. She wasn't mean…she just wasn't present; she regularly came to work mildly drunk. We didn't respect her and, therefore, didn't obey her. For some reason, one day we all rebelled, walking out the back door to our grassy plot of land vowing not to return until our mother came home. It didn't take long for every kid on that playground (as well as their mothers) to know of our mutiny. Our mother did indeed come home and gave us a sound verbal thrashing! Our responsibility was to obey the caregiver. End of story. However, it was not long after that we got a new caregiver.

My Path to Identity

Just down the street from where we lived was a small, steepled Presbyterian church. My mother had grown up in the Bible Belt, so church was a normal part of our Sunday activities. While my mother did not go to church herself as an adult, she made sure that Sunday school was part of our routine as children. This was never a "you have to," just a "this is what you do on Sunday morning." Those years of Sunday school, vacation Bible school, and sometimes church wove into my DNA a desire for God and spiritual life.

That compelling desire anchored me until my senior year in high school; it was then that I questioned the value of church. Let me backtrack a bit. Life was steady during my elementary years; we didn't have much money, but we weren't poor. It was my last year in grade school when life took a steep, downward turn. My mother remarried, just as my brothers and I were going into our turbulent teens. It was a marriage earmarked for conflict. To his credit, my stepfather took on a family with four kids. That's no small thing; but it wasn't the wisest thing. My stepfather had no idea how to parent; he only knew how to use power and intimidation to control. Fear, insecurity, hostility, and emotional abuse became our common reality…survival our common challenge. Those adolescent years, which should have been fueled by dreams, ambition, and discovery, were swallowed up by feelings of despair and futility… until my junior year in high school when I decided to try out for varsity cheer—an absolute absurdity. I was a nobody, just getting by in every sense of the word: academically, socially, and personally. But the dream was there, so I took courage and asked a varsity cheerleader to teach me the skills necessary for the job. The day came for tryouts before the whole student body. The other applicants were the popular ones; I was unknown. The other applicants performed as a team; I performed alone. When the votes came in, to everyone's amazement, including my own, I got one of the slots! That was one of the tipping points that led to a turning point in my life.

My new status gave me an open invitation to the after-game parties…parties that only the popular students attended, many of whom attended the same church youth group I attended. I went but felt awkward…unsettled…and uncomfortable with the drinking, smoking, and loose sex. It went against values that had become mine through years of Sunday school and youth group; I naively thought my youth group friends had the same values. They didn't. It was that gap between them and me that made me begin to question the value of attending church. I wondered why I was wasting my time going to

church every Sunday if it made no difference in how people who attended church lived outside of church. It's not that I felt self-righteous; I had just assumed up to that point that church made a difference in how people lived life.

It was a pivotal point that led to change: I stopped attending church…for nine months. Though short, that hiatus fostered a longing for the feelings being in church gave me: peace, a sense of belonging, the atmosphere of God's presence, and hope that there was a greater reality than my dysfunctional home life.

So, at the end of my senior year, I decided to shop around for another church, starting with a small church a classmate attended. I liked it, particularly the youth group. I felt at home and safe…even at their parties. My shopping went no further. It was in that church where I came into a personal relationship with Jesus.

I'm not sure how to explain that. I already knew Jesus. I had asked Him into my heart during a summer daily vacation Bible school program as a child, but He seemed out there, impersonal though not distant. My faith up to that point seemed more like a belief system than a personal relationship until one Sunday morning when I witnessed a seven-year-old boy being baptized. It was a solemn moment…

for the church, for him, and for me. And that's when I realized I wanted to be baptized.

I'd had an aversion to commitment at any level all my life. Intuitively, I wanted to be in control; commitment said I wasn't. But something in that moment was hallowed and sacred, and it corresponded to my inner longings for a personal relationship with the Jesus in whom I believed.

I whispered to my friend that I, too, wanted to be baptized. So, she took me to the pastor after the service.

"How can I be baptized?"

"Well, this is what you do: After the end of next Sunday's message, when I give the altar call, you walk down the aisle, and you can be baptized."

I can do that, I thought to myself, and the following Sunday, I took that walk. This small congregation was ecstatic! People came up to congratulate me, hug me, and welcome me into their family of faith.

My Sunday school teacher asked, "How long have you been a Christian?"

"Oh, I've always been a Christian!" She must have been aghast at my reply.

True to the pastor's promise, the next Sunday, I was baptized. There was no counsel, no pastoral

instruction on the spiritual prerequisites for baptism—just respond to the altar call and you're good to go. Despite the pastor's deficiency and my ignorance, that step of baptism said I was no longer my own; I belonged to Another. That changed everything for me. Jesus became personal. Church became my lifeline. I learned to pray out loud because of Wednesday night prayer meetings. I began to have hope for my circumstances.

I also longed to be a Christian witness at home. This latter was a biggie. My stepfather detested church, Christianity, and God. He had been raised by a churchgoing mother who was into law without love and a placid father who loved but didn't lead his household. At eighteen, my stepfather left home to join the navy and never darkened the doors of a church again. My starting point to witness was the simple act of bowing my head to silently thank God for my food. The first time I did this, I was so nervous my thumbs were twirling furiously in my lap.

"What wrong with you thumbs?" my young sister asked curiously.

You could have cut the air with a knife. My stepdad said nothing as I raised my head, but his stony silence said it all. He disapproved big time! But it was a start—a Christian presence had been brought into our home.

I worked at a shipbuilding company my first year out of high school. While further education had been on my radar, I didn't have the credits necessary for college nor did I have the finances. One day a youth group friend asked how my college goals were coming along.

"They're not."

"Have you ever considered a Bible school?"

I had no idea what a Bible school was, but he handed me a brochure a few days later. What piqued my interest was the cost—$600 a year! Several months later, in September 1960, I boarded a Greyhound bus to travel three days from sunny southern California to the snowbound prairies of Alberta, Canada. Prairie Bible Institute would be my home for the next five years—four years as a student and one year on staff.

As a new Christian, I needed to learn biblical truth that would form a foundation under my feet; as a person, I needed to learn self-discipline. My developing years of childhood and adolescence were so dysfunctional; I lived in survival mode… just getting by, just keeping my head above water.

I didn't learn how to study, how to keep my room clean, or how to have goals and then reach them by disciplined decisions and lifestyle. Without realizing it, I was being prepared for God's future and hope for my tomorrows.

It was during my second year at Prairie that I heard God call me to foreign mission work. The event was Prairie's Fall Mission Conference; the speaker was a missionary to Indonesia. My sense of call was not an emotional response to a stirring message. I just knew within my soul that saying "yes" to go to the mission field was the right thing to do.

That *yes* began to define what I was about going forward…the subjects I took, the clubs I joined, the organizations to which I wrote. After finishing my studies and a year on staff, I had been selected as a mission candidate for the Worldwide Evangelization Crusade (aka WEC International).

A year and a half later, I boarded a plane headed for Java, Indonesia. A month shy of turning twenty-six, I was single, had never traveled outside North America, and was naïve. I implicitly trusted that everything would go as planned. I had no idea of the unsettling experiences I would encounter before I even reached my destination!

I had routed my trip via Bangkok, Thailand, to visit a friend. The second day there, we toured the city; afterwards, she hailed a tuk-tuk to take me back to her house while she finished some office work. The driver assured her he knew the way and didn't need the written address; he didn't know the way! For hours, we went round and round the maze of streets and alleyways. We were totally lost. At some point, he got the brainwave (It must have been God!) to take me to the English Embassy; they knew my friend's organization. They called, she came, and I breathed a sigh of relief.

Three days later, I continued my journey to Jakarta, capital of Java, Indonesia. I had telegrammed my date and time of arrival so expected someone from the mission to meet me at the airport. They did not. Two hours later, a Chinese gentleman approached me.

"You seem to be waiting for someone. Can I help you?"

I explained my situation.

After thinking for a moment, he said, "I have an American friend you could stay with overnight; I'll take you there."

My Path to Identity

It was getting dark as he put my luggage in his car; and as I opened the back door, I suddenly became afraid. *Whatever am I doing? I'm getting in a car with a man I don't know in a city I don't know!* I felt trapped. *How can I not go with him? He already has my luggage. I don't want to offend him.* With fear gripping my soul, I asked God to protect me.

True to his word, this gentle Chinese man took me to his friend's apartment. "Here is the key to your room. Do not unlock your door until tomorrow morning." The words seemed ominous, but they gave me a strange sense of safety. The next morning the Chinese man returned, took me to a Christian mission organization who called my mission 800 miles away and arranged a plane ticket to Surabaya where I was met, taken to Malang, and eventually taken the next day to a small village in the hills of Batu.

I learned afterward that the mission was frantic. They knew I was arriving but hadn't received the telegram stating the details of my arrival. To put this situation in context, the country was unsettled and unsafe due to the residue of a failed Communist coup two years earlier. They had good cause for alarm! Yes, I was naïve but with a heart for God. And it is here where my journey into identity begins.

The Awakening of My Soul

Walking down the cobblestone street of our small village one morning, I realized that I was basically bothered. A year and a half into missionary life had exposed deep insecurities. To be honest, they had been there all along but camouflaged by friendships, activity, comfort zones, the familiar. I now had none of that; what I had was a new language, a new culture, a new community, a new lifestyle. I had lost everything that told me who I was; I felt alone, inadequate, and inferior.

To put this in context, my mission community was composed mostly of Indonesians and Germans; I was the only American, which had a significant impact. The Germans had their own cultural community as the backdrop for stepping into the Indonesian culture; I didn't. There was no American community to anchor me as I struggled with not only the Indonesian culture but the German expatriate culture as well.

On another front, I found the language a challenge. As languages go, Indonesian is very simple and straightforward…but you still must learn it! I discovered that I learn best with instruction and

structure in a classroom with a teacher skilled in laying the scaffolding and then building…one brick at a time. Yet here on the field, apart from a list of vocabulary words, I was expected to learn by listening.

I was doing fine until a new German worker, who was a linguist, arrived a couple of months after me. In six weeks, she was telling her story in a large conference numbering hundreds while I was still struggling to say, "Good morning"! Well, not really that bad, but still bad enough. Comparisons began to be made…by me and by others. It's not surprising that inferiority and depression became my constant companions.

As I walked down the cobblestone street that day, contemplating another three and a half years of this (the designated term from my sending organization), my outlook was bleak indeed. I knew that if I didn't find out what was wrong internally, I would either have a breakdown or go home a failure. Neither were acceptable options.

I turned to a couple who had recently transferred from India to Indonesia. They were older than the rest of us, had more experience than the rest of us, and had a spiritual vitality the rest of us didn't have.

I turned to them not because they were trained counselors (they weren't), but because they had a personal walk with the Holy Spirit…and what I needed was something more than human psychology.

For one solid year, I knocked on their door every Wednesday afternoon at two o'clock to unravel the messiness of my soul. Every afternoon was different, depending on what I was struggling with at the time. In retrospect, we covered three broad categories: unconfessed sin, personality, and strongholds of Satan.

Some of my insecurity came from sin that was buried, either through denial or blame. While it appeared to be gone, it wasn't. It lay just below the surface, influencing my thoughts, feelings, self-image, behavior, and perspectives. It was poison to my spirit, soul, and body. At that stage of my spiritual maturity, my concept of sin had more to do with the external than the internal, more actions than attitudes. The Holy Spirit was faithful to unearth what I had buried; His purpose was to bring me to freedom through forgiveness. But before I could experience that, I had to own my sin…look it squarely in the face, and say, "Yes, that's mine, totally mine; I can't blame someone else." I had to be honest with myself about myself; I had to become self-aware.

This matter of self-awareness is no small thing; it takes great courage and transparency. We often talk about self-awareness as if it is achieved simply by being self-aware. It is not. It is a journey of vulnerability beyond the destination of self-awareness itself; it goes to God, the ultimate authority to which we are accountable. In my honesty, I must also be honest with God about me, even though He already knows who I am. This honesty involves confession…owning my sin in a spirit of remorse and repentance. It is much more than an intellectual exercise of acknowledging that I sinned. My heart is genuinely sorry.

Sin carries with it guilt and condemnation. We might find ways to get around that; but when all our coping mechanisms are stripped away, these two realities stand strong and consume our souls. The only pathway to freedom is through asking for forgiveness. We need to be forgiven by a holy God against whom we have sinned. The apostle John understood that when he wrote, "If we confess our sins, he is faithful and just to forgive us our sin and to cleanse us from all unrighteousness."[1] Once I could take ownership of my sin, it was a small step to confess that before God and ask for His forgiveness.

---

[1] 1 John 1:9.

Some of my insecurity came from not understanding my personality and how it functioned in everyday life. Upon reflection, the term back then was *temperament,* and there wasn't much written on it. I've since learned that I am a number one on the Enneagram scale, a reformer. That means a whole lot of things on the positive side. I am: "conscientious, sensible, responsible, idealistic, ethical, serious, self-disciplined, orderly, and feel personally obligated to improve myself and my world." [2] But on the negative side, I am: "opinionated, impatient, irritable, rigid, perfectionistic, critical, sarcastic, and judgmental." [3] Both sides can be problematic, and both sides were! Being conscientious, responsible, self-disciplined, and obligated to improve myself and my world was challenged when I couldn't be perfect, no matter how hard I tried. I found unstructured language learning at odds with the order part of who I am. Differences in culture and personality were fodder for my critical nature; judgmentalism was the result. Being opinionated made open conversations difficult. So, I began to feel isolated, alone. It was necessary to identify my personality traits and embrace them as part of God's design in His creation of me. That which was positive, I needed to affirm; that which

[2] The Enneagram Institute (RHETI v2.5).
[3] Ibid.

was negative, I needed to let God transform. This was/is a lifelong process. As you continue to read my story, you will find this matter of personality being an issue again and again.

Some of my insecurity stemmed from not understanding the part Satan played in my struggles. To be perfectly honest, I'm not sure how much I understood about spiritual warfare at that point. Certainly, I knew there was a devil, but certainly, I didn't know how he showed up, when he showed up, or why he showed up in my struggling soul.

Depression, oppression, and anxiety were labels with which I was unfamiliar. How could I ever discern what was mine to hold and what was the work of Satan, my enemy? I couldn't at first, but over time, I began to discern his ways of working. In between my Wednesday sessions, life could go along quite nicely—no bumps, no struggling, just peace in my soul. But sometimes, I would experience heightened anxiety for no reason or fear that had no discernible cause.

The closer it was to Wednesday, the more disturbing the feelings became. Inevitably, the Wednesday session would be revelatory: we would see a core need or discover a key that unlocked a door in my soul. While I didn't like the turmoil

of those feelings, I came to understand they were signs something significant was taking place in the heavenly realm that would greatly impact my internal realm, and Satan was trying his best to hijack that holy work in me. I learned from this couple how to discern the work of the enemy, how to apply truth to his lies, how to use the power of the cross to break his strongholds, and how to walk out into freedom—a whole person.

It was a year that was intense, uncomfortable, and thorough; but one Wednesday, I walked away saying to myself, "I'll not be back." God had graciously met me in the core of my being; I felt settled and secure with me: who I am, my identity.

Looking back, I now know that my journey had only begun; many more years would be necessary to bring me to wholeness and freedom in this matter of identity.

The Mountaintop of Marriage

Two weeks after my last Wednesday of soul care, a team of twenty-one students from my Bible school and I headed to a sister Bible school in Sumatra. It was a three-day journey of 1,000 miles via train, boat, and truck. The students who were trained teachers were headed to the interior to teach in our mission's grade school for a year. I went to help Robin Hadfield, a new international worker from New Zealand, run a youth camp in that same interior for a week. To get to the interior, we had to travel another three days over pothole-covered roads, sometimes on bamboo rafts, and once walking across a swinging bridge with raging water ten feet below and only a thin pole to hang onto. The travel was three days of fun, camaraderie, and good conversation, and it was repeated one week later when the youth camp was over.

My month in Sumatra came to an end, a month that proved to be a tipping point that led to change. Two nights before heading back to Java, I was invited to the field leader's home for dinner… and who should be there but Robin! At the end of the evening, he walked me back to where I was

staying. It was a warm, tropical evening, quiet and still, just right for sitting on the steps of our campus church to talk about nothing in particular…just remembering the good times we'd both enjoyed over the preceding month.

In the middle of reminiscing, Robin asked a question that seemed out of the blue: "Do you think the Lord has a future for us together?" It was an honest question, given our mutual enjoyment of each other, but I was totally unprepared for it.

"I don't know," I cautiously replied. "I don't even know you. I don't know how you treat your mother…your sister. I just don't know you." I have no idea how the conversation took shape after that, but we did end it by deciding to pray about it for two months at which time Robin would be visiting my Java field for three months.

As I walked the few yards back to where I was staying, I couldn't get this conversation out of my mind. "What a ridiculous conversation I've just had. I don't even know him!" I said to myself. I entered the house with that statement in my head when I heard what seemed like an audible voice, "Don't you trust Me?" A simple question, but it nailed me. It wasn't whether I knew Robin but whether I trusted God. My immediate response was, "Yes, Lord, You know I

trust You. Didn't I obey You by going to Indonesia as a single woman? Of course, I trust You."

With that word *trust,* I immediately fell in love. Suddenly, I had feelings I had never had before…not even in my adolescent years. My heart started beating a mile a minute, warm feelings of longing for Robin flooded me, and I just felt overwhelmed with passion for this man I didn't know! This was so outside my realm of experience that I knew it had to be God…. He had spoken. He did have a future and hope for us together!

Because we had said we would pray for two months, I knew I couldn't tell Rob what had happened; he had to hear from the Lord himself without any influence from me. So, I returned to Java, holding hope in my heart for love and marriage. The only ones in whom I confided were the couple who had walked with me for that year of soul care, Ernie and Ede Shingler.

The two months passed ever so slowly, and Robin and I met again, this time in the Shinglers' upstairs living room over a cup of tea.

"What has the Lord said to you?" was Robin's entrance to this most significant moment.

"What has he said to you?" I answered.

"Well, nothing." In the three months of prayer, he had heard nothing from God?! I have no idea what we said after that, but again, we decided to continue holding the matter before the Lord for another month. That month passed, and we repeated the scenario.

"What has the Lord said to you?"

"What has he said to you?"

Same reply: "Nothing."

At that point, I suggested that maybe God had nothing for us together and that we should just drop it…walk away. That wasn't a good idea from Robin's perspective, and he suggested another month of prayer. So, we prayed.

At the end of that month, I held a youth retreat and asked Robin to be the speaker of the last session, a campfire ending to a good week of youth work. It was outside and off campus. As we walked to that meeting, Robin said he would like to take me out before he went back to Sumatra, which was only a few days away. I said yes, but he would have to get permission from the field leader to do so. Cultural protocol required it. My thought was, if he had the nerve to get permission, there must be something happening!

Sure enough, he got permission, and we went to Malang to a hole in the wall for great Chinese food. As I ate my delicious frog legs, he asked the same question, and I asked the same question back. He answered the same: "Nothing."

By that point, I was livid inside! Again, I have no recollection of how the conversation went…but we were scheduled to have dinner with the Shinglers on our return, a dinner that they planned to be a celebration of our engagement. There was no way we could cancel that dinner at such late notice.

As we traveled back thirty minutes by public taxi and then another twenty minutes by horse-drawn cart, I could scarcely be in the same space with this guy; in my head, I was saying, *I've had it! He's played around with my emotions long enough.* (Of course, he had no way of knowing what God had said to me and how hopelessly in love I was with him!) *I just want him out of my face and space. I want…need to get on with my life!*

I heard that still, small voice again, this time saying, "Walk in the spirit and not in the flesh." I knew God was calling me to a higher way of responding.

"Okay, Lord, I will, but I can hardly wait until he's gone."

It was afternoon siesta when we arrived at the Shinglers, so we went to our separate rooms for a rest. I picked up my scheduled Bible reading with deep inner turmoil, and this verse was staring me in the face: "A bruised reed He will not break, and smoking flax He will not quench."[4] It spoke comfort and care to my soul. God was saying He knew my turmoil and was not riding roughshod over my soul; He had this in hand, and I could trust Him.

Afternoon siesta always ends with a cup of tea, so we sat again in the Shinglers' upstairs living room with a tea tray before us three hours before the supper meal. Robin began the conversation with: "God has spoken."

"Oh, and what did He say?"

He, too, had picked up his Bible in those siesta hours and read: "Oh, magnify the Lord with me, and let us exalt His name together."[5] It was a word of direction, a word that gave him the confidence he needed to propose. But it was also a prophetic word; it told us how we would function in Christian ministry—always together. Based on that word, Robin got down on his knees and said: "Will you marry me?"

---

[4] Isaiah 42:3.
[5] Psalm 34:3.

"Yes!" Only then did I share my experience of the three months before. The supper meal was indeed an engagement celebration.

Five days later, Robin headed back to Sumatra with plans to return in May to help with the final preparations for our July wedding. It was during a picnic lunch on the hillside of a nearby resort that Robin fell in love with me. All the same emotions I had experienced months before became his to own... the passion, the longing, the out-of-control beating of his heart—all his!

It is worth noting that Robin's proposal was an act of obedience to the will of God; the emotions came later. For both of us, the will of God was the basis of our marriage. But then, it had been the will of God that led us from two different parts of the world (New Zealand and America) to the same country (Indonesia) and the same mission organization (Indonesian Missionary Fellowship). Marriage was only an extension of how we had individually been living...submitted to and directed by the will of God. Not a bad basis for marriage!

Two years ago, we celebrated our fiftieth wedding anniversary—not with fanfare, a party, and speeches, but simply an overnighter, a browse through Seattle's Pike Place Market, and an intimate dinner in the

ambiance of a long-established Italian restaurant. It reflected fifty years of doing life together…of contentment with each other…of acceptance of who we are as individuals and as a couple.

Our first two and a half years of married life were in the Sumatran Bible School. At the two-year mark, we had our son Duane, and at the two-and-a-half-year mark, we went home for our first year-long furlough. It was during that year when our second son was born, Jeremy Guy. Life was good.

A Shift through Sifting

Our furlough year was split between nine months in New Zealand and three months in the U.S. The nine months were all about pregnancy, getting to know Robin's family, and settling into his country's culture. The three months were spent introducing my husband and two babies to my family and getting plugged back into my home church, which was our main supporter.

Somewhere in that year, we both became unsettled about going back. Was it because the glamor of missionary life had worn off? Was it because we knew the reality of what we were returning to? Was it because we liked being in our own culture, speaking our own language? We didn't know, so we sought counsel from our mission leaders: New Zealand, the U.S., and Indonesia. We were looking for direction, for confirmation.

"Of course, you should go back!" they all counseled.

Our uncertainty deepened significantly through an incident with my home church one month before we were to return. We were one of the agenda items for their annual congregational meeting: Would they continue to support us? The question was not budgetary but doctrinal: did we believe in the present-day ministry of the Holy Spirit? We did; they didn't. They said they would give us time to address the issue after they had discussed it among themselves…without us in the room. When they invited us back into the room, they had already decided "no" to continuing our support.

I felt betrayed and abandoned. I felt betrayed because of the way they handled the situation and because of our relational history. They knew me. I had gotten saved in this church. I was one of their spiritual children. I felt abandoned because they stopped our support one month before we were due to return to Indonesia. How could we ever make up that level of support in our final month? We couldn't! My identity with this church was shattered.

It was January 1974 when we headed to our mission headquarters in Fort Washington, Pennsylvania, seeking direction. We had not only our own internal questioning, but now we had a substantial lack of monthly support. We also did not have a plane ticket back to Indonesia. To us, it seemed we had our answer: Don't return. However, the mission saw it differently; they paid for our return ticket. So, we boarded a French plane headed

to Indonesia, still wondering if we should be going back, and now wondering if the mission had interfered with the will of God for our lives.

What was interesting about the flight we had chosen was that it went via Viet Nam, touching down ever so briefly in Saigon; this was just three months before that city fell to the Viet Cong and communism. Hedged with weeds and overgrown grass, rusted gun placements dotted the runway. You could have cut the atmosphere in the plane with a knife. It was the silence of raw fear! A few brave (or do I say insane?) people got off; as our plane took off, you could feel the collective sigh of relief.

The destination for our second five-year term of mission work was the Bible School in Batu, East Java, specifically the children's and youth department. So, we settled into village life and my former mission community; only now the Norwegian culture had been added to the mix.

The issue I struggled with this time was one many missionary mothers struggle with: *Where does family fit into mission work? What and who takes priority—children or work? Am I a missionary first or a mother first?*

I realize now that I was in transition. Most of my first term of mission work was spent single, only the

last two years as a married woman and only the last six months as a mother. I went back to the second term as a mother of two babies. I was trying to find where I fit into this thing called missions as a mother who is also called to mission work. The struggle was within; the mission did not draw the lines.

Looking back, it was really an issue of identity: *who am I?* I think Robin also struggled, though to a lesser degree. When you don't have clear lines of demarcation, things become blurry, you become confused.

This is where we were when our six-month-old baby Jeremy became critically ill, literally overnight. He had cried piercing screams all night long, and we felt helpless to know what to do. The next morning, a staff meeting was scheduled at the school. We were expected to be there but wondered whether we should go. We wondered whether Robin should go while I stayed home with our sick baby. We wondered if we should both stay home?

Ultimately, we decided Rob should go…to get the two German doctors out of the staff meeting. By the time he returned, Jeremy was gone. We're talking fifteen minutes. We had been back on the field only three months.

Life became a haze after that; grief seemed to numb our souls, and we walked around like robots. Our mission community grieved with us, grappling to understand God's purpose and struggling to know how to comfort us. They nor we knew how to walk in such a circumstance…how to respond to God when we had reached depths within ourselves for which we had no words.

Looking back, I think, ultimately, we all let the circumstance be what it was, let ourselves be who we were, and let God be who he is—God. We didn't seek understanding or answers or closure. We just leaned into the God who had called us all and let time bring the distance we needed.

In that time-distance period, Robin and I moved out of the village house into an old Dutch villa in the university town of Malang, thirty minutes down the road. There, we started working with youth full-time: a weekly youth group in our living room, retreats, two teenage boys living with us who needed good parenting, teaching the Bible in a local Christian high school, and whatever else came along.

The interesting thing about the Christian high school was that it was the end-of-the-road high school, established for those who were failing educationally. It was situated in the downtown market area and attracted both Christians and Muslims. It gave Robin a wonderful opportunity to share the gospel message freely.

Though we had a focused purpose and had found our footing, we still felt unsettled with our call to Indonesia. The question remained: *Should we be here?* As time went on, negatives kept building up that said no: Our financial support level never improved, our youth ministry seemed to lack God's blessing, we felt like we didn't really fit in our mission community, and we were feeling more and more a desire to do pastoral work in our own culture. We continued to seek counsel, talking not only with our own mission leaders but also with the many Christian leaders who came through our university town.

During all this dialogue, we were letting God sift our motives. *Are we running away? Do we want our comfort zone? What's behind our feelings of inadequacy? Maybe we are inadequate and don't want to admit it. Are we unwilling to adapt? Is there a critical spirit in us so that we see only the negative? Do we have expectations that are more carnal than spiritual? Are we right to believe that the will of God should be fulfilling?*

At the end of four years of processing and praying, we said, "Lord, we've done everything we've known to do to resolve our unease at being here. We still

have no reason to believe we're in the right place, so we're going home to enter pastoral ministry. If we're making a mistake, then change us." It wasn't a prayer of desperation or victimization or confusion. We had reached a well-thought-through decision that needed to be brought to God. While we were at peace with where we had landed, we knew we couldn't absolutely trust our own hearts, so we needed to surrender our decision to His higher purposes. He had the authority to redirect our thinking if our thinking was wrong. He was still our God, and His will was still our priority in life.

We waited and watched to see God's movements. We experienced doors opening for us in the direction we had set. A different mission in our town wanted to start an evening church service for expatriates and asked Robin to co-pastor that ministry. He loved it…and so did all of us in the expatriate community. Those Sunday evening gatherings were springs that refreshed our souls. Another mission leader said, "Robin, you'll need a car when you return to the States; I'll have one ready from our mission's supply." Others gave financially. Our desert began to blossom as the rose; we had turned a corner.

Our original sense during that year in between terms was right, but it was necessary to go through

God's sifting process. We had to be an open book before His light; there could be no self-serving motive in leaving the mission work. Also, we needed a strong foundation under our feet that could withstand even our own struggles in concluding. At the deeper levels of our souls was an unspoken philosophy: once a missionary, always a missionary. Translation: You don't leave the mission field if you've been called. Where we picked that up, I have no idea. Did someone say it at a mission conference when we heard the call? Was it something that just evolved through our years of missionary work? We wondered, *Is it true? If it is true, what are the wider consequences of that? Does leaving mean we weren't called? If we leave, does that mean we've failed God? Can we leave and still be in the will of God?* These were challenging questions we needed to grapple with rather than bury or deny.

In retrospect, though there were many levels of sifting during that second term, the core of that sifting was around the matter of identity. Who were we? Were we confident in who we were and confident in God with who we were? I think when we reached our decision to go home, we finally were there: We didn't fit. We had tried hard to fit. Nothing in our circumstances said we fit. It was fine not to fit, but

A Shift through Sifting

we needed to go where we did fit, and we trusted God to take us there. So, a shift of where we served had been made through God's sifting process.

The Broken Years

A sweet spot in those five years of our second term was the birth of our two daughters. By the time we stepped off the plane in the U.S., we were a family of five: two adults, a one-and-a-half-year-old, a three-year-old, and a five-year-old. We had no idea what we were going to do, how we were going to support ourselves, how we were going to get into pastoral ministry, but we had one car and a place to stay! Some very good friends were spending their retirement years volunteering in Christian organizations around the States. Their house was ours for as long as we needed it.

We knew that we needed to resign from our mission organization. In the process of doing that, the U.S. headquarters asked us if we would contact a family in our area who had completed the mission's training and had been accepted as candidates for overseas missions. They had gone home to pack up their household when serious fissures began to show up in their marriage. We were asked if we'd come alongside to offer some counsel. A quick phone call ended with an invitation to attend their church the following Sunday and stay for lunch.

My Path to Identity

While sitting around their dining room table, we learned their church was looking for a new pastor. "Why don't you consider it?" they seriously asked. We did…and ended up pastoring that church for a year. We knew they had had a church split before we applied for the job; we didn't know until in the job that the congregation that had stayed was still split: the older who liked "the way things were" and the younger who wanted change. We got along well with both groups, but we were young ourselves (in our late thirties), so we wanted change too. Our immaturity and lack of church leadership experience made us poor candidates for the role we had stepped into and became ingredients for another church split, this time with us as part of the package! I'm ashamed to admit it, but we left the church and took a group with us to start another church. How can God bless that? He can't…but we had yet to find that out.

Our small group of zealous believers gradually grew. This was during the eighties and the Jesus movement—an evolution that was making headlines around the world and that had been born out of disillusionment with the hippie movement. A key couple in our group had been in the hippie movement but fell in love with Jesus and brought their hippie friends to our church. This couple was the connector to the subculture we would never be able to reach ourselves. They were a doorway that had significant influence.

We were an across-the-board-American little church: young and old, middle class and poverty line, people who knew where they were going in life and those who were trying to find life after the drugs and free sex of their hippie days. Those early days for us were happy. Love of the brethren was not something we worked at; it was just there. We liked being together and found every reason to do so—a Sunday potluck, kite flying Saturdays at the bay, nights of prayer, and celebrations to end a congregational fast. Out of choice, we lived in one another's pockets and knew when people were struggling financially, needed committed friendship to break a drug habit or help with a shaky marriage. We were members one of another, knit together—we were family. A dynamism and excitement marked our church life, a security and sense of well-being, the intimacy and transparency of trusted friendships. We were living what God intended church to be, which was thrilling and satisfying.

But if unhealthiness is at the core of anyone or anything (and starting this church the way we did was certainly unhealthy!), problems will begin to appear. So, they did: grumbling, criticism, and resistance to our leadership. We were green when we started this church, we just didn't know it. We knew mission work but not church work. We knew how to be part of a team but not how to be the leader of a team. We knew how to flow with structure that was already in place but not how to create structure that would free people to minister yet provide boundaries that would give security and sound leadership.

The day came when we heard these words from our key couple: "We feel the Lord has told us to leave." That was the start of our own church split. People began to exit in the ones and twos; not a mass exodus, but an exodus nonetheless. We were deeply troubled and confused. So, we called an all-night prayer meeting. We needed desperately to hear from God, and hear we did! At some point in the evening's quiet, God gave me a prophetic word: We were as the small boy's lunch of John 6:9. If we gave ourselves away, we would feed the multitudes; if not, we would rot. We all knew God was calling us to close our doors. So, we did.

That was the start of significant change for Robin and me: no more sermons to prepare, no more people to mentor/counsel, no more overstuffed calendars to juggle, no more community of trusted friendships, no more dreams, no more goals to reach. I stood in

my kitchen one morning looking at a blank calendar; I had nothing to do. A sense of worthlessness gutted my soul. It was then I realized that busyness had validated my sense of value, and when that was gone, my sense of worth was gone as well.

Confusion ran deep in our veins. We felt isolated and alone. One couple tried to keep our relationship going…but they and we were too wounded. We couldn't find one another, couldn't get back to what we had before: trust, transparency, acceptance. The relationship never severed, but it did change. Thanks to their perseverance, the relationship steadied, gradually growing over the years, and today, they are two of our closest friends.

No more ministry also meant no more income, which thrust us into the secular world for work. How scary that was for both of us! I had spent all my adult years in Christian ministry; Robin had worked in a bank six years before heading into Christian work. Our resumes had plenty of work experience but all in the context of Christian ministry; we were not equipped for the marketplace of secular society. That meant we had to take jobs wherever we could find them.

I became a filing clerk at the local gas and electric company and did after-school childcare. Robin

cleaned offices at night for an older man in the church we had begun to attend who had a cleaning business. Once Robin worked for a screen-printing business that produced advertising products for businesses (e.g., pens, tee-shirts). At one stretch in this journey, he sold oil paintings at home parties; on a good night, he came home having made $1,000. We passed out flyers in neighborhoods as a family. At the time this was happening, we had three kids in a Christian school and two of those kids were in braces! It was hand-to-mouth living, but we never missed a bill, never went into debt. God's provision was always there, somehow…someway.

Was this all we were worth? That question arose not from our intellect but from someplace deep down in our soul. While passing out flyers one day, a pastor we knew passed us on the street and stopped to chat. I wanted to hide or pretend I hadn't seen him. I felt embarrassed, almost guilty that we had resorted to such a lowly state of capability.

But some good things happened in this season… and perhaps because of this season. When the chips were down, our kids rooted for us, supported us with their trust, and bonded as never before. They believed in us, which gave us great comfort. Often, they would leave notes on the entryway floor where

Robin couldn't miss them when he came home late at night from a showing or cleaning offices. "How did it go? I prayed for you. I love you." The strong family unit we had been building became even stronger.

During this season, we experienced the practical care of a loving Father through His people. Once Robin came out of the bank and met a pastor friend who was going into the bank.

"I've just come into a windfall and want to give my tithe from it to you." He put $700 in Robin's hand.

That summer, we celebrated our son's fifteenth birthday. Birthdays are big things on our family calendar. Because our finances were tight, we decided to go to the beach for a campout, taking our son's best friend with us. The two of them were peas in a pod, and surfing was their delight. We came home to find $800 stuffed into our front door. Bags of groceries would sometimes be left on our doorstep, reminding us that we were not alone…not forgotten.

At one point, Robin took a course geared to help people find jobs. It was perhaps our lowest point. It assumed Robin didn't know how to write a letter, fill out an application, present himself to an employer, or write a resume; it also assumed he had few marketable skills and even less work experience. Demoralizing as it was, he hung in there until he

discovered just down the hall a small telemarketing business that needed staff! He was hired, and that led to a bigger telemarketing business forty-five minutes away. He worked there for a year and a half, calling businesses that might need his company's product of trade-show equipment. Eight hours a day, five days a week, phoning to generate orders was mind-numbing and soul-destroying, creative energy was neither encouraged nor required. In robotic fashion, just pick up the phone, go down the endless list of names, and call.

During this time, Robin began talking about going home, back to New Zealand. For twenty years, he had been away from his roots, his family. He needed to touch base with his past, his culture. I totally understood but felt we would be running away, that we hadn't learned what God was trying to teach us…not only in the present situation but why this had happened to begin with. What did we do wrong? How did we get to where we were? Why wasn't our hard work and love for God enough in the ministry?

We had many conversations around returning to New Zealand, some of them heated. One such conversation ended with Robin saying, "We are not going to talk about this again for the next two weeks.

We'll just pray." We had been praying, but this next praying would be individual only and have a decision tacked to it.

It was a Sunday when the two weeks were up, and we decided to find a quiet spot under an oak tree at Wild Cat Canyon Park in Lakeside to share what God had been saying to us. During those two weeks of prayer, I saw something in Robin I hadn't seen before: he was close to burnout. That frightened me because I knew if that happened, we would be in big trouble. He had to go home to the comfort of the familiar to find his footing again. In those two weeks, I came to his way of thinking, and we agreed! Based on that unity, we committed to going back and sealed that decision in prayer.

Two weeks later, I was frying chicken for Sunday dinner (before fried chicken was a no-no) when the phone rang. It was an elder from a church in New Zealand. We had been in contact with this church many months before, but they had gone silent on us. His words were: "Two weeks ago, the Lord spoke to us; we would like to invite you to pastor our church." Our faith had become sight…God was leading us back! We began the process of moving.

My Path to Identity

I would like to say our night of the soul was over and daylight had come, but I can't. We still had much to learn and much more brokenness to experience.

The church we were called to pastor was a small community church with people who loved the Lord and were well-bonded with each other; they welcomed us warmly. They were ready to be pastored, and we were ready to pastor. They wanted to grow, and we came with a tool that might help to that end: telemarketing! It was a new concept, and it was American, but they rallied to the challenge. Robin mobilized the congregation to connect with everyone in our suburb via phone, inviting them to our Sunday morning service. New faces began to appear, and we slowly began to grow. A new energy was rising; our Sunday morning gatherings were exciting.

But Robin and I really hadn't changed within ourselves and, therefore, really hadn't changed in how we led. We were able to pastor because we love people, have deep empathy for their struggles, and want to nurture them in every way possible. Robin was able to preach because he was gifted in that, and he valued the power of God's written word…that it holds succor, correction, direction, and relevancy to our twenty-first-century lives; but we had not learned how to lead a church or how to function in

such a way as to create followers who catch our heart and vision. We were insecure, and that insecurity negatively impacted our leadership role.

In retrospect, I realize that our leadership style was more autocratic than collaborative. I don't think we were extreme in that, but we did believe the buck stopped with us, the leaders. The outcome of that mindset was that we expected people to follow us just because we led, not because we had built a team that bought into our vision.

The first layer of followers is the elders. We stepped into the church not understanding that our priority was to bond with these two men and their families, becoming a team. To do this would take vulnerability on our part, but we were too insecure to let them into our struggles, uncertainties, and pain, particularly regarding our previous pastoral experience. We should have done that when we applied for the position…but we didn't, thinking that doing so would slam that door shut. In not being transparent, we were dishonest, manipulative, and distrustful of them and God. Transparency and trust lay a foundation on which to tackle issues together, but we didn't lay that foundation. So, when there were differences, it was hard to work through them. Four years down the track, we walked through

another church split; three years after that, we walked out of pastoral ministry altogether.

It has taken many years to get a proper perspective of all those pastoral years and experiences, to get past the blame, the perceived wrong of others, the sense of betrayal. It took years to see that our personal insecurities and leadership style (because of those insecurities) created many of our problems. Insecurity is an issue of identity, and leadership style is the fruit of that issue.

Breathing Space

While God intentionally conforms us to His image and releases us to the full potential of how we've been created, He is not a hard taskmaster in that pursuit. The psalmist David said, "For He knows our frame; He remembers that we are dust."[6] He knows our capacity and governs His workings accordingly; therefore, there are times in the conforming process when we find ourselves in respite...a breathing space.

Without knowing it, we were on the cusp of that one morning as we sat in a coffee shop in Christchurch, New Zealand, with the Avon River as our view. I had been working part-time for an organization that brought Japanese students to New Zealand to study English in our high schools. In the course of that job, Robin and I realized how our cross-cultural years in Indonesia had prepared us for this, and suddenly it dawned on us, "We could do this!" So that morning, as we sipped our coffee, we strategized on a scrap piece of paper about starting our own business, International Student Care.

The government had just opened its doors to China, and students were coming en masse. We

---

[6] Psalm 103:14.

found ourselves on the ground floor of a brand-new industry in New Zealand. The need was for homestays, help with visas, meeting students at the airport, getting them bank accounts and SIM cards for their phones, acclimatizing them to their new culture, attending parent/teacher meetings if they were high schoolers, and being there for whatever needs they or their parents had. The job description evolved as the industry grew.

At the time, Robin was still pastoring our small, struggling church, and I was heading up our new business; but there came a point I realized business was outside my bent. If it was to grow, Robin needed to get involved in its everyday workings. Then we started grappling with two realities. Our church's finances couldn't sustain us. Therefore, supplementing that income was necessary; International Student Care was the supplement. But most of our time and emotional energy was spent in the church, leaving little for developing our business.

We had arrived at a tipping point: stay at the church and limp along with the business or leave the church and grow International Student Care. We prayed, agonized, and reasoned much over that decision; the only sensible direction was to leave the pastoral ministry. Knowing when to end a ministry is just as important as knowing when to begin a ministry; however, leaving church ministry for a secular occupation is often perceived as less than the highest. It was the right decision to make, though many doubted it. We submitted our resignation.

Leaving our church left us with "Now where will we worship?" A Baptist church just fifteen minutes away was where we went the Sunday following our resignation. The pastor and his wife were Robin's friends, dating back to pre-missionary days. Then they were in teachers' college and Rob was in the bank, but they all did missions together in street evangelism and children's work with Open-Air Campaigners. When Robin went to Indonesia, they faithfully supported him/us during our ten years there.

We stepped into their church that first morning with Robin feeling a failure, ashamed, his identity shattered. Here are his words: "If what I did and accomplished was me, then me is now void." This couple knew us, valued us, and believed in us when we couldn't believe in ourselves. They were a couple ideally suited to be with us in that painful transition. We were warmly welcomed into their church and given time to heal and find our footing again; in fact, they said to us, "You don't have to do anything; just be."

My Path to Identity

That we did for more than a year, but there came a day they asked one of us to join the elder board. They didn't care which one, but one it must be! Since board meetings are more me than Robin, the choice was a no-brainer. But Robin wasn't let off the hook; he was frequently asked to share the pulpit…using his teaching/preaching gifts to enrich the church community. Gradually, we were being thrust again into pastoral leadership…but this time without having to carry the full weight of that leadership: we functioned under the lead pastor. It was the antidote to Robin's sense of failure and crushed identity.

Our business started small: one group of seven students from Indonesia and one Korean girl. In our wildest dreams, we would never have imagined that our ministry in Indonesia some fifteen years before was going to pay dividends, but it did! That group of seven came to us because we knew their culture, could speak their language, and understood the chasm between their world and ours. As time went on, we took on other nationalities: Japanese, Chinese, Malaysian, and Vietnamese. It was a whirlwind… exciting, challenging, and provisional; for the first time ever, we had money in the bank!

By this time, our son had finished university and migrated back to the States for employment. His two sisters followed suit after their university education, which left Robin and me keeping the home fires burning. We looked at each other and said, "There's something wrong with this picture!" We had always been a close-knit family, and the thought of living on our own during our later years was a nightmare that wouldn't go away!

We started praying about migrating back to the U.S. as well. Again, we found ourselves needing divine guidance...something of a supernatural quality that told us clearly the will of God. We had three big boulders before us: our business, our house, and a green card/work permit for Robin. Those boulders became the gauge for understanding God's purposes; they needed to be removed if we were to return.

The first priorities to be tackled simultaneously were our business and green card. We needed to sell our business to have the finances to resettle in the U.S. But would it sell? Because international student work was a brand-new industry in New Zealand, not enough time had gone by for the industry to establish its roots and prove viability as an income earner. No one in the industry had sold their business; we were the first.

My Path to Identity

The first thing we did was find a broker. After that, it took a year and a half to create a profile, draw up legal documents, sift potential buyers, and train the one who would carry on what we had started. However, the groundwork for that year and a half had been laid long before. For several years, we had diligently worked to build integrity, credibility, and trust with the schools and universities we serviced. At some point in this journey, Robin realized we needed signed contracts from these institutions. One by one, those contracts came into our hands. We didn't know it at the time, but those contracts were what we would be selling.

The people buying our business wouldn't be buying a business built on our personalities and the relationships we had established; they would be buying actual contracts with established institutions in New Zealand, contracts that underpinned the value of International Student Care. The broker did his job well; he found a buyer, a couple who wanted to work together, building something that would take them into their retirement years. Boulder number one was removed.

Regarding the green card, we knew it would be easier to get in New Zealand than in the States; so, I started working through the myriad of forms needed.

This was definitely outside my expertise but aligned with my bent towards detail and thoroughness. The difficulties in this task were the legal language and, at times, the seeming contradiction of expectations. In retrospect, we should have hired an immigration lawyer, but we wanted to save money. So more than once, I placed a call to the U.S. Embassy in Wellington, New Zealand, to unravel the conundrum facing me.

The day finally came when we were invited to the embassy for an interview. Despite no problems with the interview and no problems with our paperwork, Robin wasn't given a green card. The one thing they had to do, they hadn't done! We went home empty-handed, waited two weeks, then celebrated when a FedEx carrier knocked on our door needing Rob's signature. Boulder number two was removed.

With the hardest two of the three boulders behind us, we were somewhat sure that the will of God was becoming plain. However, one boulder remained: selling our home. The housing market was good back in 2004; people were buying when we wanted to sell. While our house was small and not remodeled, we were perched on an embankment overlooking hanging willow trees, banks of green grass, and the Avon River that wound its way through the suburbs

and ended in the city of Christchurch. Our house sold without much effort. I can't possibly tell you our excitement and joy—we were going to our children, who were the treasure of our hearts. The will of our good God had purposed this!

Owning our own business for ten years was our breathing space...a parenthesis from the spiritual responsibilities we didn't have the emotional maturity to handle well. It created distance that mellowed our pain and our perspectives. It also gave us the opportunity to be productive, to build something that had integrity and credibility to it. That had enormous value: We weren't complete failures after all! It provided financially; we paid off our home in eight years and saved enough for a future we were unsure of even as we saved. Owning our own business was God's mercy to us, a gift of grace that had a significant place in the transforming process of us/me.

A Piece of Paper

As rewarding as our International Student Care work was, we lacked a sense of fulfillment in it; something deep down in our souls said we weren't called to this. We weren't aware of it, but God was getting us ready for something different, something aligned with our passion. During this period of unsettledness, we attended an evening service at our church. As we sat towards the back, the speaker came up to us with these words: "Your ministry is not finished." We didn't know what that meant, but something resonated that a prophetic word had just been spoken over our lives. So, when our boulders were removed and we knew we were returning to the U.S., we wondered what lay ahead. By this time, the one thing we did know was that we were called to ministry. It was the passion of our hearts; nothing else brought meaning, purpose, and fulfillment of being.

As people became aware that we had sold our business and were moving back to the States, the two questions they all asked were, "What are you going to do when you get there? How are you going to support yourself?" We had no idea! We just knew our children were there, God was directing us there, and we would find out when we got there. But we did go back with a piece of paper, a letter of introduction to the northwest superintendent of the Christian and Missionary Alliance denomination; we knew that denomination because we attended an Alliance church when we closed our church plant. The person who wrote the reference had become a good friend through the church we attended after we resigned from our second church. He was also the head elder of our church's board and a very good friend of the superintendent, who happened to be a New Zealander! Dots were coming together. Who does that but God? "…All things work together for good to those who love God, to those who are the called according to his purpose." [7]

After landing Stateside again, we set up a lunch appointment with the district office. Because the superintendent was away for a few weeks, we met with the person in charge of church health. It was a relaxed luncheon, with good and informative conversation: if they had an opening, it would be as an interim pastor helping churches that had gone through a church split! Panic, fear, and futility gripped our being: How could we lead where we had failed so miserably? Feeling terribly disqualified, we

---

[7] Romans 8:28.

drove the four hours home, knowing we couldn't do interim work, even if it was offered. It would be a full year before we connected with the district again.

The last few weeks before moving back to the U.S., Robin began looking online for a house to buy. Through trial and error, he learned that once we found a house we liked, he had to move quickly, or it would be gone. One Thursday night, right before heading to bed, he found a house that was everything we wanted and needed: a five-minute drive from our son and daughter-in-law, ample room, well-kept with aesthetic appeal. He placed a phone call to one of our daughters that very night, asking if she would go see the house the next day with a real estate agent. They went and gave a thumbs up, so we asked our other daughter, son, and daughter-in-law to see it on Saturday. When they, too, gave a thumbs up on Sunday night, we put an offer on the house, sight unseen by us but well supported by our children, who knew what we valued in a home. Our offer was accepted. A month after landing on American soil, we moved in and began the process of unpacking, buying furniture and electrical appliances, setting up bank accounts, finding the stores and shops that would be our go-to places, establishing our rhythms and routines—everything that settling in means. It took us a year.

Then a morning came when Robin sat in his overstuffed blue chair and said, "Lord, I have nothing to do." As quick as a wink, he heard the words, "Don't worry, you will." And just a few days later, we received a phone call from the district. "We'd like to ask you to be the interim pastor for a church in West Seattle." *West Seattle…where's that?* we wondered. The church had been through a painful split and needed stability, faith, and hope for the future.

"Could you do that in three months?" they asked. We laughed to ourselves…you must be kidding! We walked into that church with no how-to manual but with a twofold agenda: listen and love. We desired to hear their stories and love them past their pain and confusion. It was a beautiful time seeing them move towards healing and hope. Nine months down the track, they were ready for a new senior pastor, and the district was ready to offer us another interim pastoral position.

So began ten years of interim pastoral ministry for five Christian and Missionary Alliance churches. Our job was threefold: preach on Sunday morning, shepherd the congregation, and troubleshoot the issues that had caused division. It required stamina, courage, making the hard calls, shouldering criticism, quiet confidence in God who had called us, and

humility. We didn't do it perfectly, and we often felt stretched beyond our gifting and capacity, but God enabled us to bring these churches to stability. We are grateful.

The nine months at the West Seattle church significantly impacted us. As we listened to and loved the West Seattle congregation, we also experienced God's healing work. We had gone back into ministry knowing we were called, but the backdrop of our failures had left its mark. We felt incompetent, unqualified, fearful. In this regard, it has taken me a long time to get my head around a spiritual principle: Failure is not a disqualification but a verification... if you've been trained by it.[8] Our past failures in ministry had equipped us to help this church and four others who had failed in ministry. Our failures were God's chiseling tool to shape us for the kind of ministry He purposed for us to have in the latter years of our lives. We were more seasoned, more leaning into God and not ourselves, more compassionate and accepting, more sure that the cross is the only answer to humanity's dilemma of brokenness. Failure was the pathway that got us there. We're not the only ones who have traveled that road. We followed Moses, David, Paul, Mark John, Samson, and Peter.

---

[8] Hebrews 12:11.

All failed…but God didn't! Joseph's comforting words to his brothers ring true: "…You meant evil against me, but God meant it for good, to bring it about as it is this day, to save many people alive." [9] Failure in the hand of God is good, not evil; He will put His stamp on it, turning its ashes into beauty. [10] So we've found it to be!

---

[9] Genesis 50:20.
[10] Isaiah 61:3.

Gathering the Pieces

In my journey of identity, the ten years of interim pastoring was the season when God gathered up all the pieces of the previous years. It was a season of self-discovery and God-discovery at a deeper level than I had known before. He started it through a book I picked up that had been on our bookshelf for years: *Boundaries* by Townsend/Cloud. I had never read the book, thinking I had no problem setting boundaries. But as I read, I realized that boundaries are more than setting limits to keep something/someone out; actually, boundaries are parameters that define who I am and what I'm about. Boundaries in life are a part of identity. That was a brand-new thought. A light bulb went on in my head, and I started to look at boundaries from the perspective of parameters. Three passages of Scripture had a profound effect at this stage of my journey: Genesis 1–3, Matthew 24:14–30, and Romans 12:3. This chapter is all about the truths in those passages that intersected with my journey in identity.

I went back to the Bible to take another look at the first parameter ever laid down for mankind, the boundary of the tree of the knowledge of good and

evil in the Garden of Eden. I had always considered that tree God's litmus test for Adam and Eve: Would they choose to obey Him? This time I saw it not as a test but as God's icon of two eternal truths: Adam and Eve are human, and they need God in that humanness. The tree was a visual that reminded them of their roots and their reality.

In their human state, Adam and Eve had it all: dominion of their world, a perfect environment, up close and personal communion with their Creator, unfettered relationship with each other, identity/value/meaning. They could answer the three great questions of life:

Who am I?

What is my worth?

Why am I here?

Yep, they had it all...except the tree of the knowledge of good and evil. The tree was something God had placed in their perfect world and declared it out of bounds, off limits. They lacked the tree, and that lack was on purpose. That lack was God's intentional design, crafted to remind man that perfect though he be, he is not God (that is his *reality*) but God's creation (that is his *roots*). The tree delineated the difference between God and man.

The ramification of those two truths is that man is neither all-sufficient in himself nor all-inclusive by himself. Man lacks, and in this lack, he needs God. He is to find in God what he needs to meet his limitedness, his lack. As man draws from God what he needs, he will continue living out from God and not out from himself. He will live life in a relationship with his Creator, which was God's design. It is the foundation and framework of the Trinity; it was to be that for humanity.

Lack is designed by God to fulfill a purpose. That truth had a serious impact on me. It changed how I saw my limitations and how I responded to those limitations. I have generally lived feeling very limited in who I am and what value I bring to life; but with this perspective, I began to see my limitations as God's parameters, designed to keep me leaning into Him to complete me.

We all live with lack in one form or another, things that are out of bounds to us, things we wish we had, things we think would complete our world. We wish we had a different job, a better home, a happier life, financial freedom, marriage (if single) or a better marriage (if married), a better start in life, a different personality, a happier childhood, a healthier or better-looking physical body. Lack is common to

us all; how we perceive that lack and respond to it determines our soul's health.

The tree, God's parameter, told Adam and Eve who they were: they were not God but creatures of His creative hand. That was their *reality* and their *roots*.

But the tree was also God's parameter that defined what Adam and Eve were about, what they were to be engaged in. At creation, they were placed in the Garden of Eden as their domain; they were to own it and occupy it, tend and cultivate it. It was their responsibility. Here they were to represent and reflect their Creator, doing so with all the creativity, intelligence, and ability God had invested in them at creation. The garden was theirs to own.

But when the serpent came to Adam and Eve, he implied that it wasn't enough, that it lacked. They believed him and sought to close the "lack gap" themselves. They ignored what was theirs to own and occupy and reached for that which didn't belong to them. They reached for the tree; but the tree was God's territory.

That thought stopped me in my tracks! I began to wonder whether Adam and Eve's problem wasn't my problem as well? That I, too, don't own and occupy that which is mine but reach for that which doesn't belong to me: someone else's fame, success, possessions, lifestyle, spirituality, gifting, blessing, personality, or whatever.

The Holy Spirit began peeling away the layers and let me see my own heart. I cringed! The list was revealing, but it was only the start. Another list ran through my mind; it was a different sort of list but just as damaging. The things on this list also belonged to another, but I took them on as if they were mine: someone else's problems, conflicts, hurts, struggles, and challenges. I thought of the times (and there many) when I had tried to close the lack gap on behalf of others, not giving space for others to own their domain (including their lack). I was Mrs. Fix-it; and in that role I played God, telling others how to live life. Essentially, I took away their right to own and occupy their garden, to take responsibility for that which had been given them. The outcome was always the same: personal conflict in relationships.

The reflection of the two lists was sobering. I didn't like what I saw, but I knew it was true. My constant longing for that which wasn't mine (the first list) or taking possession of that which was someone else's (the second list) meant I was basically an unhappy, driven woman working hard to complete my world—or perhaps more accurately, to complete

me. No matter how hard I worked, I could never quite hit the mark. You see, I was attempting to occupy territory that was not mine to occupy, and it just didn't work.

So, I began to ask myself *What am I responsible for? What am I to own and occupy?* I knew intuitively that it was me, who I am and what I'm about. It's inclusive of my body, soul, and spirit. I am to take responsibility for myself, honing areas I had left unattended and undeveloped, bringing order and beauty to the inner and outer world of myself.

That thought excited me and challenged me to roll up my sleeves and get to work. But to do that with integrity, I needed to be settled with God's creation of me; I needed to accept who I am. Only with that acceptance could I own and occupy my garden.

But self-acceptance has always been a battle for me. For most of my adult life, I have struggled to have a healthy perception of who I am. Inferiority has dogged my inner world for as long as I can remember; it seems to be part of my DNA. It ebbs and flows. Sometimes, I know very well who I am and am quite comfortable with that, thank you very much! Other times, I'm very dissatisfied with myself; it's then that I want someone else's territory to own

and occupy. Grappling with inferiority brings to the surface the gap between who we are and who we want to be.

Each time the tide of inferiority hits my shoreline, it hits me at a deeper level, and each time I grapple with it at a deeper level. This time around, I took a hard look at my parameters. To be honest, they had never been what I had wanted them to be; because of that, I had tried over the years to reconfigure my parameters or reconfigure myself. I always ended with a sense of futility and guilt—futility because I couldn't change who I am, guilt because I couldn't measure up to who I wanted to be or thought I should be.

During this process of grappling with my parameters, I was meditating on the parable of the five talents in Matthew 25:14–30. For years, I had read this parable wrongly, looking at it through the lens of equity: The talents were unequal and therefore not fair, which impaired the servant with the one talent. My faulty vision created illusions that missed the point and misappropriated blame. But one day, one phrase was the only thing I saw: "… according to their own ability." [11] That phrase is the

---

[11] Matthew 25:15.

peg on which the whole parable hangs. The master knew his servants and their capabilities. Though each had equal worth, each did not have equal capacity. The talent was according to the capability of each; therefore, the master was fair in his allocation of the talent/s.

Though not stated, each talent carried with it responsibility. The servants were to invest what they had been given. The return on investment was to be in proportion to what was invested; they were not responsible for a return that was greater than their investment. In short, the return was according to the invested talent, and the talent was according to capacity. The master gives the talent and goes on his way, leaving his servants to manage what he entrusted to them. That's the point of the parable: to do what we have been called to do with the talents we have been given. Nothing more or less is expected. Two servants performed exactly as their master knew they were capable of doing, but the third didn't. He "...dug in the ground and hid his lord's money." [12] When his turn came for accountability, he blamed the master for his lack of return. [13] The master's response

---

[12] Matthew 25:18.
[13] Matthew 25:24–25.

goes right to the heart of the problem—character: "You wicked and lazy servant…." [14] Inherent in the talent is the capacity for return on the investment according to the size of the talent. The servant was called lazy and wicked because he didn't do what he was supposed to do with the talent. His focus on his talent-lack instead of his responsibility for the talent he had been given made him a talent hoarder when he was called to be a talent multiplier. The scope of the talents was tethered to capacity, and the investment of the talents was tethered to character. The servant had the capacity to invest but not the character to do so. Capacity is God's parameters that defines the territory I am to own and occupy. It incorporates my bent, talents, weaknesses, and strengths. To take responsibility for my parameters, I must know their components.

Paul talks about this very thing in the context of spiritual gifts,[15] but its truth is also applicable in the context of identity. He says we are not to think more highly about ourselves than we should think but think soberly. We are to have a rational understanding of who we are (identity), not who we

---

[14] Matthew 25:26.
[15] Romans 12:3.

think we are or who we aspire to be or who we should be, just who we are—the good, the bad, the ugly. We are talking about something more than our behavior; we're talking about our core—that which causes our behavior. "Be sober" is a call to reality: who are we, anyway? Answering that question requires a journey into understanding how God shaped our individuality at conception and embracing that shaping as good and enough. Understanding our capacity incorporates not only what we are and what we are not, but who we are and who we are not. The what is talents, strengths, weaknesses. The who is a person formed by God and enough to fulfill God's purposes. Accepting both the what and the who will satisfy our own longing for meaning.

A lot of my disappointments in ministry have come from expectations that were outside of how I had been created. I can get so caught up with who God is and what He can do that I forget who I am and how He has shaped me. I was (and still am) a one-on-one person, more private than public, behind the scenes rather than in the limelight, with smallness not largeness as my sweet spot. When I forget all of that, I dream what is outside of God's dreams for me; that's what I did during those difficult pastoral years. I dreamed big but experienced small. I dreamed of

a flourishing ministry but experienced a struggling one. I dreamed of having a platform of influence but found few people wanted to hear what I had to say. Big never happened.

Only years later did I become thankful big never happened. I wasn't made for that kind of ministry, was unequipped for its challenges and responsibilities. It would have ruined me, and I would have ruined it. My disappointments were driven by the gap between my perceptions of my current/future capacity and the capacity God gave me. Accepting our capacity guards against disappointments, brings contentment, and protects us from the failures that come from operating outside the parameters God has designed.

I know that behind those aspirations was pride and insecurity. Pride in that I thought I had what it took if I would just work harder and pray more. Insecurity in that I needed the affirmation that bigness implies: a validation of my worth as a person. I needed it for myself, I needed it for others, and as strange as it sounds, I needed it for God so that I could be worthy of His acceptance. My dreams were birthed out of my need for self-worth and value, and so they were just that—dreams that had no substance and eventually no reality. God needed to shatter my illusions and demolish my dreams. He needed

to get me living in the real world with the real me. He did that through those pastoral years. I started to "…think soberly, as God has dealt to each one a measure of faith." Not accepting my capacity leads me to imagine a future capacity that lives up to my idea of success, driven by a lack of acceptance in the sufficiency of the capacity God has given me, and therefore, reliant on my own effort.

As I started to live out from the context of who God is and how He created me, several new things began to take shape. I began to have more discernment in what I hoped for/prayed for/worked for: Was it a pipe dream or did it align with my bent? Was it expanding or contradicting my bent? Was it within the boundaries of my God-given capacity or so far removed that it would never happen? Understanding God's nature and His design for me was freeing. It changed the lens with which I viewed everything. I flowed instead of fought, I valued what I had once devalued. I saw the alignment of my gifts and God's purpose for them.

The question in all of this is not the parameters and my response to them, but do I accept the design? It's a crucial question because self-acceptance lies in the balance.

But maybe the real issue is not "Do I accept the design?" but "Do I accept the Designer?" If we have not accepted the Designer, we will always be locked in an internal battle to accept His design—to weigh it, sift it with our own experiences, interpret it according to the measure of our spiritual maturity. "Do I accept the Designer" is a question that has its roots back in the Garden of Eden, hidden in the words "…you will be like God, knowing good and evil." [16] The words belong to Satan. To understand them, we need to backtrack a bit.

When Satan approached Eve that day, he had two purposes in mind: first, to undermine God's nature of holiness and love, and then to offer Eve something she could never have—equality with God. The serpent's conversation began with a question about what God had said about the trees of the garden, but not all that God had said about the trees of the garden. Indeed, God had said, "Of every tree of the garden you may freely eat" [17], but God went on to say, "But of the tree of the knowledge of good and evil you shall not eat, for in the day that you eat of it you shall surely die." [18] That part Satan left out.

---

[16] Genesis 3:5.
[17] Genesis 2:16.
[18] Genesis 2:17.

While Satan's beginning question to Eve was not a denial of what God said, it was deceptive because it wasn't the whole truth of what God had said; instead, it was a half-truth. That half-truth brought into question God's holiness and love. In essence, "If God promised you every tree yet is denying you the tree of the knowledge of good and evil, He lied; if He is denying you this one tree, He doesn't love you."

Eve answers Satan's question but adds something to the narrative: "And the woman said to the serpent, 'We may eat the fruit of the trees of the garden; but of the fruit of the tree which is in the midst of the garden, God has said 'You shall not eat it, nor shall you touch it, lest you die.'" [19] God did not say, "nor shall you touch it." It seems like such a little thing, doesn't it? But it was a deviation from truth, and that's never a small thing. Holiness is all about what is true. Eve's deviation from truth set her up for what was to follow: a full-blown lie. "You will not surely die. For God knows that in the day you eat of it, your eyes will be open, and you will be like God, knowing good and evil." [20]

What did Satan mean by "you will be like God"? What does "knowing good and evil" have to do with

---

[19] Genesis 3:2–3.
[20] Genesis 3:4–5.

"being like God"? First, weren't they already like God by virtue of being made in His image? [21] They were, but they were unlike Him in that God knew both good and evil. [22] They didn't. They knew good at the experience level because they knew only God who is good and had lavished upon them the abundance of His goodness. They did not know evil. They had an awareness of evil because they knew it was wrong to eat of the tree God had prohibited. But awareness is not experience, and it was the experience of evil that took it from intellectual knowledge to personal participation in evil's nature.

"Knowing good and evil" has to do with being able to determine what is good and what is evil, what is right and what is wrong. Because God is holy and love, He is the only one qualified to make that determination. Now here's the thing: Satan's insinuation behind his words was that once Adam and Eve added evil to their experience, they would be able to make that determination themselves because they would be equal with God. They, too, could determine what was good and what was evil. They could make their own rules, live by their own will, be dictated by their own passions. They could be self-

---

[21] Genesis 1:26–27.
[22] Genesis 3:22.

determining, living out from themselves instead of living out from God.

When we struggle with our design, when we question whether we may be missing out on something better, we are struggling with the Designer. At the core of that struggle are these questions: *Is He really good, and does He really love me?*

There was a point in my journey into identity when those questions were front and center. Our circumstances were very difficult and had been for a very long time, which precipitated me having thoughts I had never had before. *What have I been doing all these years serving God? Have I been wasting my life in Christian ministry? Where is God? Why doesn't He do something?*

These thoughts led to other thoughts: *Maybe God doesn't exist. Maybe I've believed a lie all these years. If He does exist, He must be powerless to help me or He must not love me because, if He did, He would change my circumstances.* Once those thoughts formed, it was only one small step to decide to walk away from God, but internally not externally. We had three kids who loved Jesus; I didn't want to jeopardize their faith because my own was in crisis. So, I kept this to myself (not even telling Robin) and continued with the externals: going to church, reading my Bible, praying. But I was hollow inside.

For several months I discredited God as a reality; but I realized I couldn't be rational and think He didn't exist—all creation was a living expression of a Creator. But I didn't believe He was love and, therefore, I didn't believe He loved me. Then one day I read: "But without faith, it is impossible to please Him, for he who comes to God must believe that He is and that He is a rewarder of those who diligently seek Him." [23] That's exactly where I found myself: I believed that God is, but I didn't believe He is a good God who rewards those who obey Him. The severity of my circumstances had stripped away everything I had believed Him to be.

At that point, I decided to read the Bible with this question at the forefront: *What is God like?* As I searched from that perspective, I read a constant theme: He is love. Simple, straightforward. Was I going to believe that, or was I going to believe what my feelings and circumstances told me? I realized my feelings and circumstances were unstable, subject to change and contradiction. I desperately needed something solid, something that wouldn't change. I needed a rock under my feet that would stabilize me.

---

[23] Hebrews 11:6.

My Path to Identity

One day, I told God: "I take Your word as true; though I don't feel You love me, I trust what Your word says…that You are love and, therefore, You love me. Even if life never changes, even if this is all there is, you are God, a good God, and I choose to trust You." There was no fanfare, no fireworks, just a surrender and commitment to truth. It took time, but gradually our circumstances did change, God did open doors, and a new future began to unfold.

Timing is everything. Our perception of God's goodness will rise and fall with our present experience of it unless it is rooted outside of time and circumstance. Our perception of God cannot be dependent upon our current situation. We will at times falter and at times flourish, yet God's nature is constant; it is this rock of understanding that will uphold our faith.

When we struggle with God, we think the problem is He who designed us, whereas the problem is us thinking that we are God and, therefore, know what is best for us. When everything is said and done, is not that the core conflict of humankind? Is He God and will we willingly submit to Him as God? Or are we god, ordering our lives under that delusion and demanding God do things our way?

In the face of that question, I had my answer to inferiority: God is God, and I am me. He as God created me just as He wanted me to be, and that design is perfect because He is perfect. I no longer need to measure up to my own expectations of who I think I should be because who I am is exactly who I should be. I can live within my garden with freedom, owning and occupying the territory that belongs to me. Self-acceptance put a whole new dimension to life for me. I no longer lived under the shadow of "I'm not good enough; I must try harder." I could live being who I am; in God's eyes, that's enough! God-acceptance released in me self-acceptance.

But there was a nagging question that stayed at the periphery of my consciousness: Is self-acceptance a wall or a door? Is it an end or a beginning? I've known people who have said: "This is how God wired me," implying no need to change—no need to look at the traits that trip them up, attitudes that don't reflect the God who wired them, behavior that stresses their relationship with others. I couldn't buy that. Indeed, my wiring is a God-thing, but how I live within that wiring is a me-thing, for which I am responsible. Putting the whole responsibility on God didn't sit right. Oh, I liked the comfortable posture that says, "It's God's fault, blame Him," but I was

uncomfortable with its outcome: it prohibits change. And change is often what is needed.

When self-acceptance means I don't have to change, then it has become a wall, a dead end with no place to go, no hope for a future that's better than the present. I needed something better because, though I had accepted myself, I still struggled with who I am. Just like the conversation with the serpent, awareness is not the same as experience. I was aware of how God created me: my capacity and His gifts/talents. I accepted the Designer and His design, but I wrestled with my experience of it. I just didn't like certain things I saw within myself: I am insecure and, therefore, defensive and self-protective; I am self-righteous and, therefore, judgmental and harsh; I am proud and, therefore, find it difficult to hear criticism and rebuke.

These are sins of the soul and spirit, far more toxic than sins of the body. They impact my relationships, perceptions, responses, attitudes, and behavior; they influence how I think and process life, how I shape my life, and where I'm heading in life. These sins have no place in the life of a believer, yet they were very much a part of who I was. I didn't like it one bit!

I had worked hard over the years to change or reconfigure myself, but it didn't happen. I just

couldn't change. I could make superficial changes; but did I have internal change that changes outer behavior and lasts? Absolutely not!

This struggle here was as pivotal as my struggle with inferiority, though perhaps more crucial because it reflected a fundamental flaw in my relationship with God. But I couldn't get to the flaw without traveling the road of self-realization and futility. I had to discover the discrepancy between my spirituality and my actuality, between what I desired to do and what I did. I also had to experience the futility of trying to change me.

My struggle was the same one the apostle Paul agonized over: "…For I don't do the good I want to do, but instead do the evil that I don't want to do…."[24] I could have all the spiritual desires in the world, but my flesh and blood reality where I really lived life was something very different. There was a gap between my actuality and my spirituality, and I could do nothing about it. I was at an impasse.

Paul goes on to say, "…But if I do what I don't want to do, I am no longer the one who is doing it, but it is sin that is living in me.[25] I felt nailed by Paul, not only in terms of my conflict, but in its

---

[24] Romans 7:15.
[25] Romans 7:19–20.

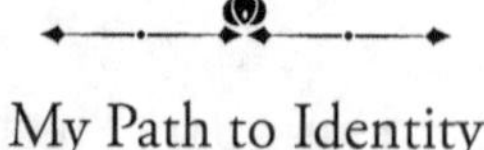

cause—sin. Not acts of sin, but a sin nature that is me. Paul says I'm a sinner.

For some reason, that hit me right between the eyes! I saw myself in a new light. This is not about me as a sinner who needs to be saved but about me as a saved sinner who is still a sinner by virtue of my inner nature. This isn't about what I do (sin) but about who I am (a sinner through and through). I'm never going to be anything else. The very fabric of my inner being is riddled with this disease called sin. Because of that, in my own power, I'm never going to be who I should be as a believer, never going to get it right or be right no matter how hard I try.

How had this truth escaped me all the years of my Christian life? I had lived knowing I need forgiveness for what I do, but I finally realized I need forgiveness for who I am: a flawed human being who has no capacity by myself to please a holy God. Yet I had tried down through the years to do so! I labored to be more self-disciplined, be more devoted, read my Bible more, pray more, be more spiritually minded, serve more, love more, be humble. This behavior which should have been the natural response to a loving God, for me, was behavior designed to get something from God: approval and acceptance. I had accepted the capacity God had given me; but as a saved sinner, I will never be able to achieve perfection a hundred percent of the time. It is a losing battle. I attempted to do more of what was in my control in an effort to control what was outside of it.

I was appalled! Paul's futility was my own: "O wretched man that I am! Who will deliver me from this body of death?" [26]   I detested who I was but found myself unable to change. I had reached a wall. That is just where God wanted me, because that wall pushed me to the same place it pushed the apostle Paul—to God. Paul finishes his cry with these words: "I thank God through Jesus Christ our Lord!" [27]

The answer to my sinfulness was not self-improvement, good works, or spiritual endeavors. I would never be able to "do" enough or "be" enough to bridge the vast chasm between God's holiness and my sinful nature. The answer was Jesus. It isn't what I do that gains acceptance by a holy God, but what Jesus did when He died on the cross for my sin. My wretchedness needs atoning, and no amount of work on my part will do that. His death paid the price for *who I am* as well as for *what I've done*. All He asks of me is that I accept His finished work. That is the

---

[26] Romans 7:24.
[27] Romans 7:25.

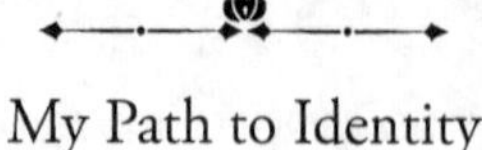

only thing I have to do to be approved and accepted by God. The Bible calls that acceptance by God "grace"—God's unmerited favor.

Was this a new truth? Had I never heard it before? Had I never believed it before? No; but this truth is not revolutionary until it becomes personally revolutionary. It became that through the journey of self-discovery: seeing myself for who I really am. All the layers of spirituality needed to be peeled away, leaving only my raw core exposed. It was necessary to see my ugliness and deficiencies. As long as I lived as if they didn't exist, or blamed another, or excused myself as "this is just me," or covered my blemishes with self-work, I would always be inadequate, always reaching for that which isn't mine.

Behind all the reaching and striving is the raw need for acceptance. The need isn't wrong because we were created by God already accepted; but sin changed that relationship, alienating us from God's acceptance. [28] My own good works, as spiritual as they appear, can never find acceptance by God. Seeing myself for who I am was necessary if I was to discover God for who He is—a God of grace who thoroughly knows me, wonderfully loves me, and gloriously accepts me…because of Jesus.

---

[28] Colossians 1:21.

Those words "because of Jesus" are used so casually in Western Christianity that I cringe when I use them myself. They need to be unpacked from a truth perspective rather than from a soul perspective—that is, how they make me feel. So, hear me out as I go back again to the beginning of all things.

From before time, [29] the Trinity knew creating man would be problematic. Their perfect intentions would be challenged and thwarted by God's archenemy, Satan, and God's very character of holiness and love would be put to the test. Man would sin, and that sin would require retribution. But how could a loving God punish? That's the question, isn't it? It's a fair question if God were only love, but He isn't. He is also holy, and it is that holiness that is the issue in retribution—not love. To understand retribution and love, we need to understand holiness. That is where we must start if our words "because of Jesus" are to have meaning and authority.

The term *holy* is two-pronged in its definition; it reflects God's transcendence and purity. As a transcendent being, God is separate from mankind, set apart. He is a different kind of being; we could say he is *Other*. He is His own kind, so far removed from us that we have nothing to which we can compare

---

[29] 1 Peter 1:19–20.

Him. He exceeds the created world and all that is in it, including mankind. In fact, He is in a world all His own, and we have absolutely no capacity to comprehend it. Bible writers have tried to articulate it; consider the apostle John in Revelation 1:12–15 or the prophet Ezekiel in Ezekiel 1:26–28 or Paul in Colossians 1:15–16 or Luke in Luke 9:29 and 32.

Glory and majesty are words mankind uses when attempting to explain God's otherness, but we have lost the sharpness of their meaning due to the commonness of their use. If we go back to their Hebrew/Greek origins, we discover a vista of superlatives: beauty, grandeur, dignity, honor, splendor, power, wealth, authority, fame, riches, magnificence and excellence in form and appearance.

If this is some measure of the definition of what it means for God to be holy, a being set apart from His creation, is it any wonder that when God presented Himself to the people of Israel in the Old Testament, an awesomeness always struck trepidation and reverence? [30] We read of those manifestations and can view them as God flexing His muscles, demonstrating His power, but that is not what is taking place. Such manifestations are but a reflection of His essence, of

---

[30] Exodus 19:16.

who He is. This God who is descending on Mount Sinai is the:

- One who has no beginning or end of days yet created time: moments, days, years, ages.

- One who is housed in infinity, who has no limits yet created space and boundaries.

- One who made something out of nothing.

- One who is invisible yet makes that which is seeable and, thereby, makes Himself known.

- One who is the uncreated Cause.

When we approach Him, we are coming to One who is beyond us, not only in terms of space but also in terms of being. A Being different in kind and scope. He is the apart One, the holy One.

In the everyday nitty-gritty of life, how does God's apartness (transcendence) connect with you and me? Are there ramifications that impact us at the practical level? I think there are. I would like to mention two:

1. There are times in life when we need something outside ourselves to run to, a shelter that is outside our storm. We need a sanctuary that is untouched by human hands, something distinctly "other." We need the personal space that otherness gives us—personal space away

from what is embroiling us at the moment. That personal space and God's distinctiveness give us objectivity; we need that. We need the inner strengthening that comes when we approach the "Rock who is higher" than our human world.[31] The realities of life make God's transcendency crucial for you and me. God, in all His apartness, stands as a shelter, a tower, a tabernacle because He stands in all His distinctiveness as holy God.

2. Not only do we need the sanctuary that God's transcendency brings, but we also need the worship that God's transcendence allows. When we recognize God's majesty and splendor, our humanness is awed by His apartness, and we know in the very fabric of our being that he is God—and so, we worship, we bow the knee. Such worship is appropriate in the Creator-created relationship, but it is more than that. Recognizing God's greatness is to have a sober opinion of my humanness—and that is good. Worship says, "I am not God; there is a Being bigger and greater than me." The power of that realization is that it brings me to a place of inner security and

---

[31] Psalm 61:2–4.

rest. David and Isaiah said it well: "Be still and know that I am God."[32] "In returning and rest you shall be saved; in quietness and confidence shall be your strength."[33]

It is God's transcendency that gives validity to our worship. We bow our knee not to an idol we have created, not to something we can control, but to One who is over all and in all and through all, One who works all things after the counsel of his own will."[34] This is the God we worship. When we do so, we discover that worship is a stabilizer, a wellspring of confidence and hope, a renewer of the inner man. When we worship, pessimism gives way to hope, futility to fruitfulness, failure to victory, negativity to faith, darkness to light. A life-giving flow is happening through the act of worship. We need that! In God's apartness, we find refuge and we find worship. *Holy* means *apartness*.

As a pure Being, God is spoken of in Scripture as being light. The apostle John lays that foundation, and James builds upon it. John says, "God is light and in Him is no darkness at all."[35] James says, "Every

---

[32] Psalm 46:10.
[33] Isaiah 30:15.
[34] Ephesians 1:11.
[35] 1 John 1:5.

good gift and every perfect gift is from above, and comes down from the Father of lights, with whom there is no variation or shadow of turning." [36] Both apostles are confronting doctrinal error that crept into the early church. For John, the error was a redefining of sin; and for James, it was that God tempts man with evil. Both apostles sought to establish a right understanding of the character of God. Man's understanding will determine man's character, and man's character will dictate man's conduct. The issue is crucial to the redemptive purposes of God: Will God's people be God's holy nation, reflecting His light in character and conduct? This is what God is after. This is why Jesus went to the cross. He died that we would become a reflection once again of our Maker. Both apostles state irrevocably that God is light in whom is no darkness at all.

When John and James talk of light, they are referring to two aspects of God's being; they are talking about the character of God and the conduct of God. God's character is absolute purity. Nothing in His being is less than radiant whiteness—no spot, no blemish, nothing that would cast even the slightest shadow. We find no discordant quality. He has no questionable motives, self-centeredness of

---

[36] James 1:17.

thinking, meanness of spirit. He is the quintessence of everything that is good.

As God's character is pure and undefiled, so His conduct is without fault. His actions are the outer workings of His inner nature and can only be consistent with that nature. God does what is right because His inner being is right. Wrong is outside the realm of possibility in God's workings because of His pure and upright nature. So, what He does is good and perfect. He doesn't manipulate, force, or deal deceptively. He's honest and upfront. He won't go back on His word. He is true to His own nature. God is pure in both character and conduct.

What does this mean to us who are living in an age where absolutes are unacceptable, where the distinctions between Christian and non-Christian are at best hazy and at worse non-existent, where we Western Christians are close to losing our way because some of our concepts about God are founded more on feeling than on fact, more from the soul than from the Spirit?

I would like to mention three truths that are relevant to you and me:

- The purity of God means that He can't wink at sin even though He loves us with everlasting love. He is a God of purity as well as passion,

a God of truth as well as a God of mercy. We need to remember that when we're tempted to live by a loose moral code, to fit into an environment that has no absolutes, to cheat on an exam, to rob an employer of time, to lie. We need to remember that if love is more important than truth in our relationships, love without truth will always lead to compromise.

- The purity of God means that God is not punitive. When bad things happen to us, they are not necessarily from God first of all; secondly, if they are God's discipline, they are intended to correct not to punish. God is not out to get even, to retaliate. There is no meanness in Him that would seek to hurt us as we've hurt Him or pay back in equal measure. God's purity is concerned only for our good, and His disciplines are to that end. He wants us to experience what is good; if something in us needs adjustment to make that happen and discipline is required, then He disciplines—but always for our good and never for evil or punishment. We need to remember that the next time we're in the throes of bad things happening, when life falls around our ears, when it seems the sun will never shine again, when we shake our fists at heaven and cry,

"Where are You, God?" We need to remember that when we're tempted to think, feel, or say "God is punishing me." We also need to remember that we are people who strive and struggle to be perfect. Perfectionism can have its roots in pride, but it can also have its roots in fear: "If I am not perfect, God will punish me." God does not call us to perfection but to excellence. Excellence is within our grasp; perfection is not.

- The purity of God means that He can give us only good things. His desire is that we enjoy all that is good and nothing that is evil. He created us to know the fullness of joy, freedom in living, the passions and compassions of love. He intended that we have life and have it more abundantly. [37] We need to remember that when we have longings that go unmet, dreams that are always elusive, a promise from God that remains unfulfilled. We need to remember that when the world looks more inviting than our Christian faith, when our feelings say, "Anything fun in life is outside my Christianity." We need to remember that when the hardness of life makes God look like

---

[37] John 10:10.

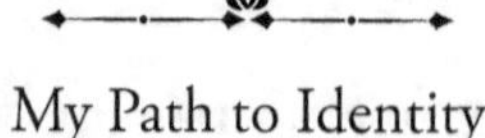

a hard taskmaster, when we don't understand what He's doing and why He's doing it. God is good and gives only good things. He is pure.

My own experience has been limited in this matter of encountering God's holiness; but when I have, awe and reverence are the only words that explain the experience and the emotion. In the presence of holiness, my sinfulness is worthy of wrath and judgment.

Getting back to Genesis, so it was that day in Eden. God spoke judgment on Adam and Eve. God's holiness required justice for Adam and Eve's sin. There was no grace, no sentimentality; just holding them accountable for their arrogance, for thinking they would equal Him. God could not wink at man's sin as if it were trivial; to do so would make His holy nature trivial. Holiness demands retribution: punishing the wrongdoers to bring justice. That punishment was death[38]—body, soul, and spirit. God is holy.

God is also love. It is because He is love that the Trinity determined that judgment wasn't to be the final word; mercy was. The apostle James said it well: "...Mercy triumphs over judgment."[39] Father, Son,

---

[38] Romans 6:23.
[39] James 2:13.

and Holy Spirit made a way for man to escape the punishment of death: a blood sacrifice could atone for man's sin. Before the foundation of the world, the Trinity planned that Jesus would be that sacrifice. He would take man's guilt and judgment upon Himself and be man's substitute.[40] Jesus would be the demonstration of God's love as surely as judgment was the demonstration of God's holiness. In His holiness, God required a blood sacrifice. In His love, He sent His son to be that sacrifice.

Jesus' sacrifice would accomplish several purposes: satisfy the just demands of a holy God,[41] cancel man's sin,[42] turn away God's wrath,[43] destroy the power of Satan, and break his authority over mankind.[44] "Because of Jesus," because of what He did, God can show mercy and grace to me, a sinner by nature.

The realization of that in my soul was profound. For the first time ever, I could stand before a holy God without appeasement, guilt, or shame. I could stand naked with no pretense, pride, or defense. I could acknowledge I rightly deserve His judgment

---

40 1 Peter 1:18–20.
41 Hebrews 9:13–14.
42 Colossians 2:13–14.
43 1 John 4:10.
44 Hebrews 2:14–15.

but could appeal to His mercy—"because of Jesus." The flaw in my relationship with God was thinking too small of Him and too big of me, thinking holy God could be appeased by sinful me.

I find in our current Christian culture we've taken holiness out of the gospel message because love is more palatable, less offensive. But we can't understand God's love if we don't understand His holiness. It is because He is holy that judgment was required, and it is because He is holy love that He sent Jesus to die on a cruel cross to take that judgment. Love is costly. [45] When love is void of sacrifice, we have mere emotionalism and sentimentality. This kind of love isn't sustainable for the long haul and can't change us where it counts—internally.

So, the question needs to be asked, "Did I change? If I did, how did that change happen?" I did change, but I need to tell you how that happened before I can tell you what that change looked like. It took realizing I am a sinner who will never be anything else before I could reach out to take God's mercy as my entrance into a new way of relating to Him—not by my own good works but his…past in redemption and present in renewal. [46] Embracing the finished

---

[45] 1 John 4:10.
[46] Titus 3:5.

work of the cross invites Jesus' life to reign in me by the indwelling Holy Spirit. As I yield to Jesus' power and authority to work change in me, He will address every trait, attitude, wound, hurt, rebellion, and reaction that is destructive to how He made me—in His image. It is Jesus in me who works internal change so that I reflect God's image in how I live life and relationships. Accepting God's gift of grace started me on that journey of transformation.[47]

So, where am I changing? I'm changing how I see others because I've changed how I see myself. Jesus talks about this in the Sermon on the Mount when He talks about the speck in another's eye.[48] Seeing myself for who I am has been to "see the log" in my own eye: those things in me that have clouded my vision of someone else. Often, the problem is not another but me:

- My insecurities make me feel threatened by someone else.

- My woundedness misinterprets another's actions.

- My fear throws suspicion on another's motives.

---

[47] Colossians 1:27.
[48] Matthew 7:3, 5.

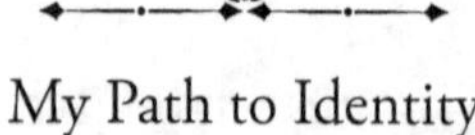

- My unforgiveness keeps the hurt from another raw in me.

When I respond to the workings of grace in me, I see others differently. What was a plank before is now only a speck. Because it is only a speck, it is inconsequential. I overlook/forgive the speck, giving grace. The apostle Peter defines it as "…love covers a multitude of sins." [49]

I am changing in how I see the irritants of another: they are God's tools for refining me. Often when the behavior of another pushes my buttons, it is because there is something in me that can be pushed, a vulnerability that is open to being wounded. God wants to illumine and change that something because it is destructive. The problem is me, not them. Understanding that gives me a different view of the irritant. I see it as God's gift, and that changes my attitude towards the person behind the irritant. King Solomon understood how growth takes place when he penned: "As iron sharpens iron so a man sharpens the countenance of his friend." [50] Growth (spiritual, emotional, mental) that takes place in me because of another's irritants is valuable beyond the irritant. I've learned to appreciate and embrace that tool and the process for my own development.

---

[49] 1 Peter 4:8.
[50] Proverbs 27:17.

I am changing to have compassion for another who rubs me the wrong way. Their blemishes and deficiencies are no greater than my own. They also are lost sinners needing grace that will change the attitudes and behaviors that make our relationship difficult. As I found grace, so can they. Paul states this very truth when he says, "Therefore, since we have…received mercy, we do not lose heart."[51] My own discovery of grace gives me hope; as grace was there for me, it is there for the person with whom I struggle. I need to let God bring them there just as He brought me there.

I am changing in my focus: I am responsible for me—my garden, not another's. I am to own my own stuff, making confession and asking forgiveness from God and the person with whom I am in conflict. Their stuff is for them to own. I can release myself from that, allowing God to bring them to that same place of grace where they can take ownership, asking forgiveness when necessary. Paul says it this way: "If it is possible, as much as it depends on you, live peaceably with all men."[52]

I am changing my perception of the power of the cross. It is the only answer to my sinfulness and the sinfulness of another. As the blood of Jesus covers my

---

[51] 2 Corinthians 4:1.
[52] Romans 12:18.

sin and breaks its power, so it does for the one with whom I have conflict; therefore, when we confess our sin to God and one another, it is forgiven, and we can walk in fellowship with one another again. [53]

I am changing in the matter of conflict resolution. Because I have taken care of my subjective part in the conflict, I can enter conflict resolution with an objective mind and attitude. I no longer go towards that dialogue defensive, guarded, wounded. I can go to deal with the objective facts rather than the subjective feelings.

My journey in identity has led me to grace. Along the way, I've settled the capacity issue. Life lived within my God-given parameters is a life easy to live. There's time and energy for God's purposes with enough left over to smell the roses! As it relates to all the nuances of being human, that will be the ongoing work of redemption. I'm at peace with that. Identity is the evolving work of the Holy Spirit in me. The more I find my worth and value in what Jesus did on the cross, the more I know who I am. The more I become secure in that, the more I become like Him—created in His image.

---

[53] 1 John 1:7.

✦ ── • ──❦── • ── ✦

One Last Thing

I have written little on the matter of spiritual warfare, i.e., Satan's part in my struggles; that's not because he wasn't there but because the issue wasn't him. The issue was me—my inner core that based my outer conflicts. Satan had nothing to do with that inner core—I did. However, he used the vulnerabilities of that inner core to wreak havoc and cause distress. Until those vulnerabilities found their answer in Jesus, Satan had substance that gave him the right to have authority in my life.

I find a naivety and falsehood in our Christian mindset regarding the place of Satan in our seasons of onslaught. In Jesus' final discourse with His beloved disciples, He says this: "I will no longer talk much with you, for the ruler of this world is coming, and he has nothing in Me." [54] Jesus is referring to the cross, which is only hours away, and clarifies that the reason for the cross is not found in Himself. It is not anything in Him that gives the ruler of this world authority over His life and circumstances.

This is not so with us. The ruler of this world does have something he can use against us: our sin of

---

[54] John 14:30.

wanting to be God. His power and authority over us are lodged right there—in our self-rule. He uses that something with vengeance. He lies, he accuses, he afflicts. The naivety is to blame our conflicts on the attacks of the enemy, Satan. The falsehood is to claim innocence. If we have not brought God into our core and allowed Him to minister truth and love wherever there is self-rule, then the fault is ours. Because of that, it does no good to rebuke the enemy, to change how we think about ourselves, to claim God's positivity over us; we must instead remove from Satan's hands that which allows him to target us. We must rob him of his right over us. The only way to do that is through the route of self-discovery, God-discovery, and relinquishment of self-rule to God-rule. That is our own personal journey of crucifixion. This is what the apostle Paul was talking about when he said very succinctly: "I have been crucified with Christ; it is no longer I who live, but Christ lives in me, and the life which I now live in the flesh I live by faith in the Son of God, who loved me and gave Himself for me." [55]

While we begin our Christian life by trusting in Jesus (faith), chasms deep within us are unsubmitted to the rule of God. Unless we have been convinced

---

[55] Galatians 2:20.

at the emotion and will level of our soul (not just our intellect) that the citadel of self is only destructive, we remain our own god living by our own self-rule. It is here in the chasms of self that an illumination of wanting to be "as God" must dawn on our consciousness. The tools the Spirit uses to do this divine work will be the negatives of life: disappointments, relationships, woundedness, pressures, financial stress, health issues, unfulfilled expectations, unanswered prayer, closed doors, etc. The Spirit's illumination is an invitation to come under God's authority. It involves confession and repentance, and results in forgiveness and freedom. This is the redemptive work of the cross in our inner being. This is Paul's "…It is no longer I who live, but Christ lives in me…." Our response to the negatives in our lives will have two outcomes, depending on the path we choose: one leads closer to Christ, and the other entrenches Satan's right in us.

It is crucial we understand the power of this moment as it relates to the authority of Satan over our lives. In the previous chapter, I mentioned several results from the sacrifice of Jesus: satisfy the just demands of a holy God, cancel man's sin, turn away God's wrath, destroy the power of Satan, and break his authority over mankind. When we crucify

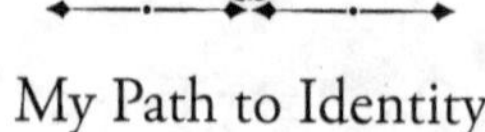

(put to death by renouncing) self-rule, a transfer of power occurs—new ownership, new authority, and a new way of being.

Paul says it this way: "If anyone is in Christ, he is a new creation; old things have passed away; behold all things have become new." [56]   Some look upon this as happening when we accept Jesus' sacrifice as payment for our sin; others see it as a crisis moment in our journey of faith. I look upon it as a multitude of moments in the journey of life—God traveling down my chasms with truth and love to bring me to wholeness of being, to the "…all things have become new." In every chasm where I deal with me and make God my God, I deal a death blow to Satan's authority over my life.

This is powerful in its practical outworking. Satan can no longer lie to me. In her book, *Lies Women Believe,* [57] Nancy Leigh DeMoss does an excellent job of categorizing then listing the lies that undergird our thought processes. You've already read some of the lies I've had to address:

God isn't real.

---

[56] 2 Corinthians 5:17.
[57] Nancy Leigh DeMoss, *Lies Women Believe,* Moody Publishers, 2001.

He doesn't love me.

I am of little value.

I have to earn God's acceptance.

I'm not enough as God created me.

Allow me to also share some of the lies from DeMoss's list:

- I should not have to live with unfulfilled longings.

- God can't forgive what I have done.

- I'm not fully responsible for my actions and reactions.

- A career outside the home is more valuable and fulfilling than being a wife and mother.

- I have to have a husband to be happy.

- If my husband is passive, I have to take the initiative or nothing will get done.

- If I feel something, it must be true.

- I can't control my emotions.

- If my circumstances were different, I would be different.

These kinds of thoughts are seen as part of our humanness; we don't realize they originate from

Satan who is the father of lies. [58] We will understand them as lies only when we understand truth.

So, let's talk about truth for a moment—in two arenas: objective Biblical truth and subjective heart truth. First, we must define truth. Truth is that which lines up with reality. The dictionary defines it as that which is correct or factual, or the state of being true. It is an exactness to actuality—no embellishment, no exaggeration, no add-ons, no subtractions. Truth is the bedrock of solid fact.

In light of that, what is objective Biblical truth and subjective heart truth? The Bible is Biblical truth. It is God's written Word to mankind. It is true because God is true and cannot lie. [59] It is objective because it is true by itself. It is true whether we feel it is true; it is true whether it has been validated by someone's experience. Subjective heart truth is the real me in my inner space, the reality that exists deep down inside. It is what I am at the core of my being—not who I want to be, not who I should be, not who I appear to be, but who I am.

Let me give you some examples of negative subjective heart truth: fear, anger, control, bitterness, guilt, blame, lust, hate, jealousy, and envy. We'd

---

[58] John 8:44.
[59] Numbers 23:19; Hebrews 6:18; Titus 1:2.

like to believe none of that is part of who we are as believers in Jesus; but if we haven't let the cross work deep within, some of those things will be there. What we do with this subjective truth will determine whether we understand the lies we buy into and whether we're able to break those lies with Biblical truth to walk out into freedom and wholeness.

It's important to understand that Satan's lies have value because they appeal to something inside of us. Our own inner reality is what gives validity to Satan's appeal; and because of that inner reality, we buy into his lie. Let's look at some Biblical examples.

- The prodigal son[60] —At the core of his being was the desperate drive for independence, to do his own thing and be his own boss. So, he bought the lie: *You have the right to your own inheritance.* We know where that lie took him: a squandered inheritance, abandonment by his friends, and a pigpen for a home.

- The Samaritan woman[61]—She needed value and self-worth to have a sense of significance and meaning. So, she bought the lie: *Marriage gives that because it gives identity, self-esteem, and respect.* That lie led to five husbands and,

---

[60] Luke 15:11–32.
[61] John 4:1–26.

ultimately, living in adultery with a man to whom she was not married.

- Ananias and Sapphira[62]—They desired to look spiritual, appear generous, and have a reputation of dedicated devotion. So, they bought the lie: *Just appear to contribute all the proceeds from the sale of your land.* They schemed to acquire a reputation for a virtue they did not possess. Authentic devotion didn't exist at the core of their being. That lie culminated in God's wrath and judgment, and both were struck dead.

- Jacob[63]—He wanted the position of the firstborn. So, he bought the lie: *The birthright and your father's blessing are your right.* That led to conniving and deception. The result was a brother who sought to kill him, twenty years of exile, a mother he never saw again, and slavery to a man far more skilled in the art of deception than himself.

- Miriam and Aaron[64]—They desired power and position. So, they bought the lie: *You should be equal with Moses.* That lie led them

---

[62] Acts 5:1–11.
[63] Genesis 25:27–34.
[64] Numbers 12:1–15.

to challenge Moses' leadership which resulted in God's anger and judgment: Miriam was struck with leprosy.

In every case, the inner reality (negative subjective heart truth) was the fabric to which Satan appealed. Without the inner condition, there would be no appeal. Without the appeal, Satan had no way to tempt. Before we can identify the lie, we must first identify our negative subjective truth. If we don't bring our subjective heart truth into alignment with objective Biblical truth, we are opening the door for Satan to use that lie to bring about destruction in our lives.

King David once wrote: "Behold, You desire truth in the inwards parts, And in the hidden part You will make me to know wisdom." [65] This is a declaration of something David learned very painfully: God is after inner truth. David's moral failure with Bathsheba and his murder of Uriah, her husband, were the direct results of lust, greed, and deceit in his inner space.

When we bring our inner stuff to God in confession and repentance, we are doing three things: we are owning our belief in the lie, we are choosing to believe truth, and we are breaking the power of

---

[65] Psalm 51:6.

the lie with truth. All three are necessary. What does that look like? Let me tell you a story.

Years ago, a friend came to me wanting prayer for deep inferiority that was destroying her life and ministry. While in prayer together, I thought *How's her relationship with her father?* It turns out she had a great relationship with her dad. He loved her, she loved him—but she always felt she couldn't please him. *That's strange,* I thought to myself. *Why was that?* Well, he had wanted a boy for his firstborn, and she was a girl. All her life she had tried to be the boy her father had wanted. Of course, she couldn't, so she always felt inadequate and like a failure.

I took her to Psalm 139 and God's design in creating her female. Through our conversation, she saw where the core of her inferiority lay: the lie that she had to be a boy to have value. As we went back to prayer, she brought to the Lord the lie and her father's part in the lie; but the turning point came when she took ownership of the lie. The problem was not her dad, but her; *she* had believed the lie. She confessed to that, repented, and accepted herself as God had created her—a female who was "fearfully and wonderfully made."[66] She walked out of that

---

[66] Psalm 139:14.

prayer time a free woman and went on to experience significant power in her ministry.

When we confess and repent of our sin, God forgives us and cleanses us. [67] We are made right with him, and there's no inner stuff to which Satan can appeal. Repentance takes the power out of sin. In that place of redemption, we can then rebuke the enemy, begin changing how we think about ourselves, and believe God's positivity over us—all based on the truth of what Jesus has done for us and in us.

It is this "in us" that gives us our testimony—our very own experience of redemption, not just a doctrine of redemption. According to Revelation 12:11, our testimony is one of the weapons that defeats the enemy of our soul: "And they overcame him by the blood of the Lamb and by the word of their testimony, and they did not love their lives to the death." While this verse is written in the context of the last days, its truth is applicable to our here and now. Confession, not denial, and the blood of the Lamb cancels the power of sin and the ability of the enemy to accuse and torment us. In case you haven't realized it, when Satan accuses us, there's always an element of truth in what he says; and that's what

---

[67] 1 John 1:9.

stymies us. Our internal tendency is to deny the accusation or blame something/someone else. The path to freedom is to agree that the accusation is true but no longer relevant—because the blood of Jesus has covered it with atoning power. It is our daily and progressive word testifying to truth that affirms our place of victory.

Does that mean that our fight with Satan is over? No, but now we fight from a different vantage point. Now we fight from the victory of the cross in our lives. It is that "in our lives" that is crucial. The cross has no power if it is only a doctrine; but when it changes us, then we have a testimony that becomes a weapon in our hands against the enemy of our soul.

A third weapon is mentioned in Revelation 12:11: "…and they did not love their lives to the death." The thought here is that of martyrdom—dying for our faith. I would like to talk about that word *death* for a moment to gain a deeper appreciation of the quality of faith that empowers one to die for their faith. When we think of death, we usually think only in terms of the body—physical death. But man does not cease to exist after the body dies; physical death is not the end. The Bible tells us that after our body dies, we will stand before a holy God to give an account of how we've lived our lives and be judged by that. [68]

---

[68] Romans 2:12–16.

It is this accounting moment that subconsciously weighs on our souls. I say *weighs* because we know we fall short of God's holiness. [69] I say *subconsciously* because this knowledge of judgment is written on man's inner being, his heart; it is there whether we believe in God or not. Hebrews 2:14–15 tells us that this weight is fear, and it holds mankind in bondage. This fear of death has been Satan's weapon over mankind ever since the garden days when its first mention was in God's prohibition to Adam: "But of the tree of the knowledge of good and evil you shall not eat, for in the day that you eat of it you shall surely die" [70]—spirit, soul, and body. They ate, so we die physically to then face the judgment of God.

It is here that we see why death is Satan's weapon. Satan has the power of death in his hands because he stands before the judgment seat with his list of true accusations in hand, [71] demanding that holy God give sinful man his just punishment of death. He is right on both counts: God is holy, requiring justice; man is sinful, deserving punishment. But Jesus' death stands starkly between the Judge and the accused; the cross affirms God's holiness while it pays man's debt. Satan is robbed of his weapon, death wrestled

---

[69] Romans 3:23.
[70] Genesis 2:17.
[71] Revelation 12:10.

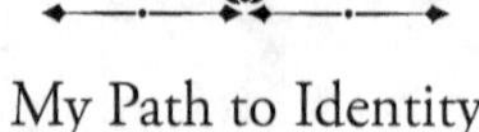

from him through death—Jesus' death on the cross. When that cross has done its own thorough work in us, then physical death no longer holds fear. Fear of physical death is stripped of its power because Satan was defeated at the cross by the cross.

We know physical death is the gateway to eternal life with the One we've come to love. Let me again quote the apostle Paul: "For I am persuaded that neither death nor life, nor angels nor principalities nor powers, nor things present nor things to come, nor height nor depth, nor any other created thing, shall be able to separate us from the love of God which is in Christ Jesus our Lord."[72] Satan is a defeated foe. Fear of death can no longer hold us captive to his power. Again, Paul said it well: "O death, where is your sting; O Hades, where is your victory?"[73]

Now, how does this last weapon connect to all that I've written on identity? Through the journey of seeing ourselves for who we really are and God for who He really is and living under His rule, we become transformed into the person God created us to be. Our identity finds its rootedness and definition in God and not in self. When we're no longer about

w

self-preservation, we're free to give our lives away. "…They did not love their lives to the death." That's the potential.

I'm not saying I'm there but finding my identity in Jesus has certainly brought me closer. It's been a long-lived journey. There are no quick fixes in this matter of becoming what we were created to be. God is in no hurry, nor should we be. So, wherever you are on this road of identity, take heart, my fellow sojourner. It is worth the trip!